JUMBLE
Journey

It's Not the Destination, It's the Jumbles!

Henri Arnold,
Bob Lee,
Mike Argirion,
Jeff Knurek, &
David L. Hoyt

TRIUMPH
BOOKS

This book is available in quantity at special discounts
for your group or organization.

For further information, contact:

Triumph Books LLC
814 North Franklin Street
Chicago, Illinois 60610
Phone: (312) 337-0747
www.triumphbooks.com

Printed in U.S.A.

ISBN: 978-1-62937-549-6

Design by Sue Knopf

Contents

JUMBLE®

Unscramble these four Jumbles, one letter
to each square, to form four ordinary words.

OSPOT

EBBIR

GRANDO

TRUXAS

DIPPING YOUR BREAD
INTO GRAVY MAY
BE BAD MANNERS —
BUT IT'S CERTAINLY
ALSO THIS.

Now arrange the circled letters to form
the surprise answer, as suggested by the
above cartoon.

Print answer here " ⬡⬡⬡⬡ ⬡⬡⬡⬡⬡ "

JUMBLE®

Unscramble these four Jumbles, one letter to each square, to form four ordinary words.

YARAR

LAVEG

MYDOBE

RUVESS

A MAN WHO CLAIMS HE NEVER MAKES A MISTAKE ISN'T THIS.

Now arrange the circled letters to form the surprise answer, as suggested by the above cartoon.

Print answer here

JUMBLE®

Unscramble these four Jumbles, one letter
to each square, to form four ordinary words.

MEPOT

EATAB

TRAUGI

LESPEN

Doesn't
look
like
much

A BIKINI NEVER
ATTRACTS ATTENTION
UNTIL SOMEONE
DOES THIS.

Now arrange the circled letters to form
the surprise answer, as suggested by the
above cartoon.

Print answer here

JUMBLE®

Unscramble these four Jumbles, one letter
to each square, to form four ordinary words.

SOGEO

USAME

YARVOS

HUBLES

IN THESE VERY
WORDS HE TOLD
HIS WIFE WHO
THE BOSS WAS.

Now arrange the circled letters to form
the surprise answer, as suggested by the
above cartoon.

Print
answer
here " ◯◯◯ ' ◯◯ THE ◯◯◯◯ ! "

JUMBLE®

Unscramble these four Jumbles, one letter
to each square, to form four ordinary words.

TAUID

CERDY

MYNITE

ROBRAW

THAT LONELY GUY
ROBBED A BANK
JUST SO HE COULD
FEEL THIS.

Now arrange the circled letters to form
the surprise answer, as suggested by the
above cartoon.

Print answer here " ⃝⃝⃝⃝⃝⃝ "

JUMBLE®

Unscramble these four Jumbles, one letter
to each square, to form four ordinary words.

BOMUG

RARBI

KRODEF

THORCC

SHE CAN DISH IT
OUT, BUT CAN SHE
DO THIS?

Now arrange the circled letters to form
the surprise answer, as suggested by the
above cartoon.

Print answer here

JUMBLE®

Unscramble these four Jumbles, one letter
to each square, to form four ordinary words.

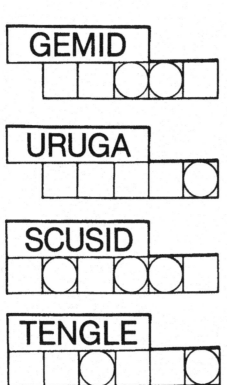

GEMID

URUGA

SCUSID

TENGLE

Here's your new regimen

WHEN THEY REACH
MIDDLE AGE, MANY
PEOPLE ARE
REDUCED TO THIS.

Now arrange the circled letters to form
the surprise answer, as suggested by the
above cartoon.

Print answer here ⬡⬡⬡⬡⬡⬡⬡⬡⬡

JUMBLE®

Unscramble these four Jumbles, one letter to each square, to form four ordinary words.

HOACC

LEKAN

RITAUN

VODURE

She looks lovely, but...

Shhh!

THE BEST WAY TO TELL A WOMAN'S AGE IS WHEN SHE'S THIS.

Now arrange the circled letters to form the surprise answer, as suggested by the above cartoon.

Print answer here

9

JUMBLE®

Unscramble these four Jumbles, one letter
to each square, to form four ordinary words.

MYDUP

CHEEN

BRUBRE

GREFOT

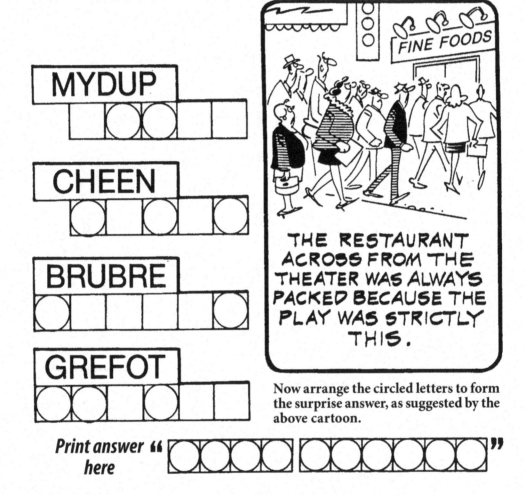

FINE FOODS

THE RESTAURANT
ACROSS FROM THE
THEATER WAS ALWAYS
PACKED BECAUSE THE
PLAY WAS STRICTLY
THIS.

Now arrange the circled letters to form
the surprise answer, as suggested by the
above cartoon.

Print answer "⬡⬡⬡⬡ ⬡⬡⬡⬡⬡⬡"
here

JUMBLE®

Unscramble these four Jumbles, one letter to each square, to form four ordinary words.

OMBOL

FONTE

DRUSAB

MUGLEE

He never acts that way at home

WHAT KIND OF PERSONALITY DID THAT CHAMPION FENCER HAVE?

Now arrange the circled letters to form the surprise answer, as suggested by the above cartoon.

Print answer here A " ◯◯◯◯ " ◯◯◯

JUMBLE®

Unscramble these four Jumbles, one letter
to each square, to form four ordinary words.

LAINF

SOMEO

LETHAH

NYFLOD

Take your gifts and get out!

Ordinarily,
he's very
smart

WHAT A MAN IN
LOVE SOMETIMES
SHOWS GREAT
INGENUITY IN MAKING.

Now arrange the circled letters to form
the surprise answer, as suggested by the
above cartoon.

Print
answer
here
A ☐☐☐☐ OF ☐☐☐☐☐☐☐☐

JUMBLE®

Unscramble these four Jumbles, one letter
to each square, to form four ordinary words.

KORBO

YADDD

RADIOT

SELAMY

They
love
to hiss
him

THAT BELOVED
MOVIE VILLAIN
WAS SO GOOD AT
BEING THIS.

Now arrange the circled letters to form
the surprise answer, as suggested by the
above cartoon.

Print answer here

JUMBLE®

Unscramble these four Jumbles, one letter
to each square, to form four ordinary words.

NICCY

DAMEF

LARREB

PARTUB

HOW THE
BACKSEAT DRIVER'S
HUSBAND DROVE.

Now arrange the circled letters to form
the surprise answer, as suggested by the
above cartoon.

Print answer here

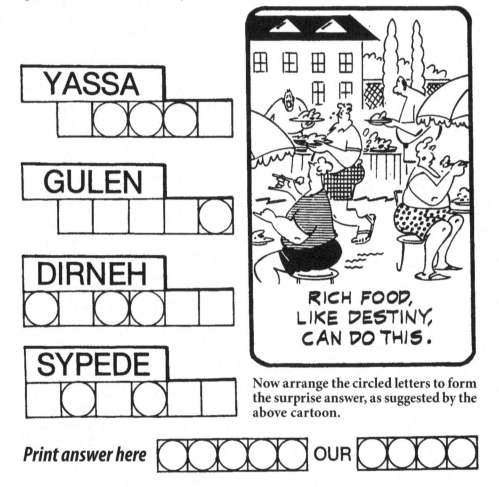

JUMBLE®

Unscramble these four Jumbles, one letter
to each square, to form four ordinary words.

YASSA

GULEN

DIRNEH

SYPEDE

RICH FOOD,
LIKE DESTINY,
CAN DO THIS.

Now arrange the circled letters to form
the surprise answer, as suggested by the
above cartoon.

Print answer here ⬡⬡⬡⬡⬡ OUR ⬡⬡⬡⬡

JUMBLE®

Unscramble these four Jumbles, one letter
to each square, to form four ordinary words.

FODOL

TELIT

DUBUSE

GENJAL

I could...

But then again, I
could also save
my money

RACING

HOW TO ASSURE
THAT YOU DON'T
LOSE MONEY AT
THE TRACK.

Now arrange the circled letters to form
the surprise answer, as suggested by the
above cartoon.

**Print answer
here**

⬡⬡⬡⬡ ⬡⬡⬡⬡'⬡ ⬡⬡

JUMBLE®

Unscramble these four Jumbles, one letter to each square, to form four ordinary words.

WHAAS

HATIF

NOPPIL

COTESK

RICH RELATIVES LEFT HIM A YACHT, AND EVER SINCE HE'S BEEN TALKING ABOUT THIS.

Now arrange the circled letters to form the surprise answer, as suggested by the above cartoon.

Print answer here HIS " ☐☐☐ ☐☐☐☐ "

JUMBLE®

Unscramble these four Jumbles, one letter
to each square, to form four ordinary words.

UNFYN

PUMBY

KUEBER

OTHPRY

WHAT HAPPENED
WHEN NYLON
STOCKINGS WERE
FIRST INTRODUCED?

Now arrange the circled letters to form
the surprise answer, as suggested by the
above cartoon.

*Print
answer
here*

THERE " ⬡⬡⬡ " ⬡⬡ ⬡⬡⬡⬡
WAS A

JUMBLE®

Unscramble these four Jumbles, one letter
to each square, to form four ordinary words.

GYANT

DANAP

GURFEE

PURROA

A GOOD HAM-
BURGER IS MADE
FROM THIS.

Now arrange the circled letters to form
the surprise answer, as suggested by the
above cartoon.

Print answer here THE ⬡⬡⬡⬡⬡⬡ ⬡⬡

19

JUMBLE®

Unscramble these four Jumbles, one letter
to each square, to form four ordinary words.

ODITI

UNDOB

CHEPSY

HOMAFT

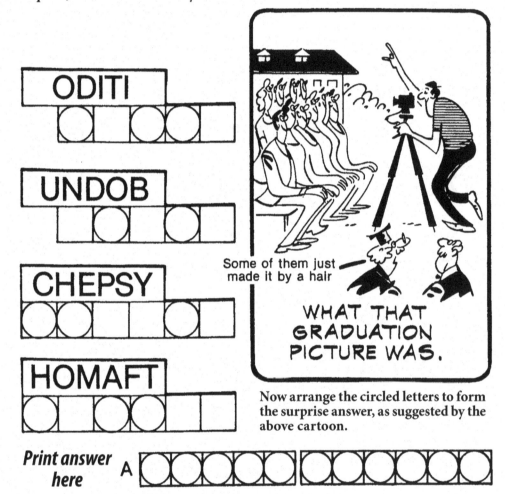

Some of them just
made it by a hair

WHAT THAT
GRADUATION
PICTURE WAS.

Now arrange the circled letters to form
the surprise answer, as suggested by the
above cartoon.

*Print answer
here* A

JUMBLE®

Unscramble these four Jumbles, one letter
to each square, to form four ordinary words.

REVNY

MOCEA

WEABER

ASHIMP

WHEN PRICES
"SOAR"---

Now arrange the circled letters to form
the surprise answer, as suggested by the
above cartoon.

Print answer here ⬜⬜ ⬜⬜⬜ ⬜⬜

JUMBLE®

Unscramble these four Jumbles, one letter to each square, to form four ordinary words.

PAWMS

NEEMY

THALEC

PHOONC

THERE'S A STRANGE DRIP IN THE BASEMENT. SHALL I CALL THE PLUMBER?

Now arrange the circled letters to form the surprise answer, as suggested by the above cartoon.

Print answer " ☐☐ , ☐☐☐☐ ☐☐☐☐ ! "
here

JUMBLE®

Unscramble these four Jumbles, one letter
to each square, to form four ordinary words.

ZIERP

ORNED

RACCES

MADAKS

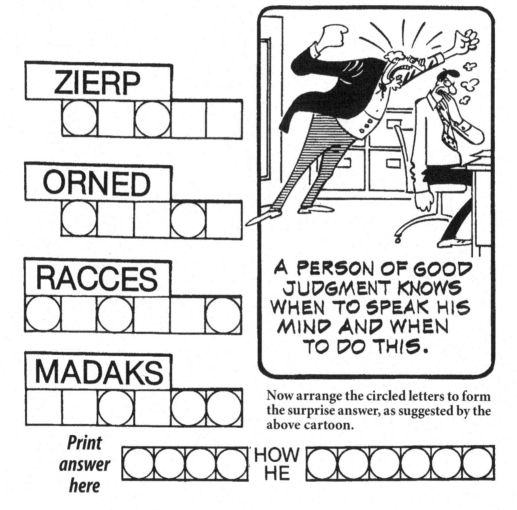

A PERSON OF GOOD
JUDGMENT KNOWS
WHEN TO SPEAK HIS
MIND AND WHEN
TO DO THIS.

Now arrange the circled letters to form
the surprise answer, as suggested by the
above cartoon.

Print
answer
here

HOW
HE

JUMBLE®

Unscramble these four Jumbles, one letter
to each square, to form four ordinary words.

KEDAB

NACAL

POUDIM

GINGON

WHAT THE JOB
OF DELIVERING
PARCELS SOME—
TIMES IS.

Now arrange the circled letters to form
the surprise answer, as suggested by the
above cartoon.

**Print answer
here**

◯ ◯◯◯◯ - ◯◯ ◯◯◯

JUMBLE®

Unscramble these four Jumbles, one letter to each square, to form four ordinary words.

SHWIK

GUCOH

TRENGY

HOKOUN

This is where you get off

REDUCING SALON

I should have gone directly to the office

IN ORDER TO PLEASE HIS WIFE, HE RELUCTANTLY AGREED TO GO THERE.

Now arrange the circled letters to form the surprise answer, as suggested by the above cartoon.

Print answer here ☐☐☐ OF "☐☐☐☐☐" HIS

JUMBLE®

Unscramble these four Jumbles, one letter
to each square, to form four ordinary words.

KEHRI

LAMDY

RAKNEC

DABBIE

I mustn't gossip so much

THE ACROBAT WAS
THE ONLY GUY WHO
KNEW HOW TO TALK
ABOUT HIMSELF---

Now arrange the circled letters to form
the surprise answer, as suggested by the
above cartoon.

Print
answer
here

⬡⬡⬡⬡⬡⬡ HIS ⬡⬡⬡⬡
OWN

JUMBLE®

Unscramble these four Jumbles, one letter
to each square, to form four ordinary words.

YARCS

FIRRA

SIBUHL

GARAVE

WHAT CAME BETWEEN
THOSE TWO POETS
TURNED PROFES –
SIONAL BOXERS?

Now arrange the circled letters to form
the surprise answer, as suggested by the
above cartoon.

Print answer here " ◯◯◯◯◯◯ "

JUMBLE®

Unscramble these four Jumbles, one letter to each square, to form four ordinary words.

NALTS

GERME

FAERRY

DOAZIC

Those songs were popular around the time we got married

Everything was much better then

ANOTHER NAME FOR NOSTALGIA.

Now arrange the circled letters to form the surprise answer, as suggested by the above cartoon.

Print answer here " "

29

JUMBLE®

Unscramble these four Jumbles, one letter
to each square, to form four ordinary words.

KEWOA

LIPTO

TERVOX

ENDOTE

HE COULDN'T SWIM
A STROKE, BUT
HE KNEW THIS.

Now arrange the circled letters to form
the surprise answer, as suggested by the
above cartoon.

*Print answer
here* EVERY " ☐☐☐☐ " IN ☐☐☐☐

JUMBLE®

Unscramble these four Jumbles, one letter
to each square, to form four ordinary words.

CIEPE

YANDS

LYNKIG

PANMEC

Did he
learn
anything
else?

THEIR KID'S COLLEGE
EDUCATION SEEMED
TO BE JUST THIS.

Now arrange the circled letters to form
the surprise answer, as suggested by the
above cartoon.

Print answer here

JUMBLE®

Unscramble these four Jumbles, one letter to each square, to form four ordinary words.

NILEN

LUNNA

RENOCE

MOSHAN

WHAT THAT BLACKGUARD WAS.

Now arrange the circled letters to form the surprise answer, as suggested by the above cartoon.

Print answer here A ⬜⭕⭕⭕⭕ WITHOUT " ⭕⭕⭕⭕ "
A

JUMBLE®

Unscramble these four Jumbles, one letter to each square, to form four ordinary words.

INWET

KICCH

FRIMIN

HELBED

At least she's doing something about it

SHE WENT TO SOME LENGTH TO CHANGE THIS.

Now arrange the circled letters to form the surprise answer, as suggested by the above cartoon.

Print answer here

33

JUMBLE®

Unscramble these four Jumbles, one letter
to each square, to form four ordinary words.

RAFIE

OAPIN

AGGIZZ

EMFONT

He doesn't know what
he's talking about

LIKE A SHIP, SOME
SPEAKERS TOOT
LOUDEST WHEN
THEY'RE THIS.

Now arrange the circled letters to form
the surprise answer, as suggested by the
above cartoon.

Print answer here

JUMBLE®

Unscramble these four Jumbles, one letter
to each square, to form four ordinary words.

LODDY

KNOTE

EXVONC

DIALIN

Maybe he can
help us out

WHY THE JURY
ASKED TO SEE THE
ACCUSED SAFE-
CRACKER AGAIN.

Now arrange the circled letters to form
the surprise answer, as suggested by the
above cartoon.

*Print
answer
here* THEY
WERE ⬡⬡⬡⬡⬡ " ⬡⬡⬡⬡⬡⬡⬡ "

35

JUMBLE®

Unscramble these four Jumbles, one letter
to each square, to form four ordinary words.

URYMM

ENMOY

BEGBIT

NURTHE

WHAT MIGHT TOM
DO WHEN HIS CAR
BREAKS DOWN?

Now arrange the circled letters to form
the surprise answer, as suggested by the
above cartoon.

Print answer here ⟨ ⟩ " ⟨ ⟩ "

JUMBLE®

Unscramble these four Jumbles, one letter
to each square, to form four ordinary words.

OTTOH

ZYZID

NOBBIB

EXCOIB

YAK YAK
YAK YAK

AN "ADDICTION" TO
THIS CAN CAUSE
SOME PEOPLE TO
BECOME SLEEPY.

Now arrange the circled letters to form
the surprise answer, as suggested by the
above cartoon.

Print answer here " ◯◯◯◯◯◯◯ "

JUMBLE®

Unscramble these four Jumbles, one letter
to each square, to form four ordinary words.

YEMSS

SURVI

DOHOKE

CRESIB

WHAT THAT
AMOROUS PITCHER
KNEW HOW TO
THROW BEST.

Now arrange the circled letters to form
the surprise answer, as suggested by the
above cartoon.

Print answer here ☐☐☐☐☐☐

JUMBLE®

Unscramble these four Jumbles, one letter to each square, to form four ordinary words.

ENFEC

MEPIR

TOEGEA

ODONEL

WHAT MIGHT GO ON INSIDE A COMPASS?

Now arrange the circled letters to form the surprise answer, as suggested by the above cartoon.

Print answer here " ☐☐☐☐☐☐ ☐☐☐☐☐ "

JUMBLE®

Unscramble these four Jumbles, one letter
to each square, to form four ordinary words.

YOPPP

SUMOE

MISTEK

NUCLUR

HE WAS SO DULL
THAT EVERY TIME
HE LEFT---

Now arrange the circled letters to form
the surprise answer, as suggested by the
above cartoon.

Print answer here THE ◯◯◯◯◯ ◯◯◯◯ ◯◯

JUMBLE ®

Unscramble these four Jumbles, one letter
to each square, to form four ordinary words.

DYKEE

SOUHE

TEECIX

YURFIP

HER APPEAL
SPRANG FROM THIS.

Now arrange the circled letters to form
the surprise answer, as suggested by the
above cartoon.

Print answer here ◯◯◯ " ◯◯◯ ◯◯◯ "

41

JUMBLE®

Unscramble these four Jumbles, one letter to each square, to form four ordinary words.

DABIE

ACTUD

ROYLOP

BONECK

Looks like we're going to have great fishing

Don't bet on it

WHAT THE SKEPTIC'S OUTLOOK IS.

Now arrange the circled letters to form the surprise answer, as suggested by the above cartoon.

Print answer here A "  "

JUMBLE®

Unscramble these four Jumbles, one letter to each square, to form four ordinary words.

BOESE

RUSUY

SYMFIL

YUBILS

THE ONLY SURE WAY OF CATCHING THE NEXT TRAIN IS TO ---

Now arrange the circled letters to form the surprise answer, as suggested by the above cartoon.

Print answer here ◯◯◯◯ THE ONE ◯◯◯◯◯◯

JUMBLE®

Unscramble these four Jumbles, one letter
to each square, to form four ordinary words.

VURCE

BLEEL

GOYAVE

WHOSAD

WHAT A FILIBUS-
TERING POLITICIAN
SHOULD DO.

Now arrange the circled letters to form
the surprise answer, as suggested by the
above cartoon.

Print answer here " ⃝⃝⃝⃝⃝ " HIS ⃝⃝⃝

JUMBLE®

Unscramble these four Jumbles, one letter
to each square, to form four ordinary words.

NUMOR

BEREL

SMABAL

LEUXED

You shouldn't have

THAT EXOTIC
PERFUME
HELD HER---

Now arrange the circled letters to form
the surprise answer, as suggested by the
above cartoon.

Print answer " ◯◯◯◯◯ ◯◯◯◯◯ "
here

45

JUMBLE®

Unscramble these four Jumbles, one letter
to each square, to form four ordinary words.

THEIG

ISTOC

HANEEV

GLEINT

A HORSE IS
WHAT MORE PEOPLE
BET ON---

Now arrange the circled letters to form
the surprise answer, as suggested by the
above cartoon.

Print answer here

JUMBLE®

Unscramble these four Jumbles, one letter
to each square, to form four ordinary words.

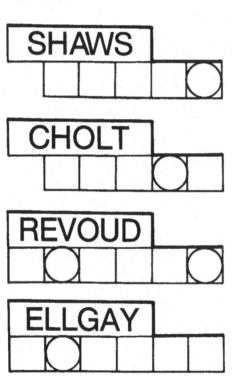

SHAWS

CHOLT

REVOUD

ELLGAY

MORTGAGES
ASSESSMENTS
TITLES
CLOSINGS

IN THE REAL ESTATE
BUSINESS ONE LEARNS
THAT THE BEST IN-
VESTMENT ON EARTH
IS USUALLY THIS.

Now arrange the circled letters to form
the surprise answer, as suggested by the
above cartoon.

Print answer here

47

JUMBLE®

Unscramble these four Jumbles, one letter
to each square, to form four ordinary words.

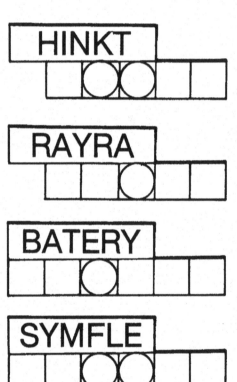

HINKT

RAYRA

BATERY

SYMFLE

He's trying to embarrass them

THE WORST FAULT
OF AN INDISCREET
GUY IS TELLING
OTHER PEOPLE---

Now arrange the circled letters to form
the surprise answer, as suggested by the
above cartoon.

Print answer here

48

JUMBLE ®

Unscramble these four Jumbles, one letter to each square, to form four ordinary words.

NOWNK

WULAF

FOLFAY

PEKAUM

I'm m-m-making no deshisions at thish time

Time to go home

HE FOUND IT EASIER TO SIT TIGHT THAN THIS.

Now arrange the circled letters to form the surprise answer, as suggested by the above cartoon.

Print answer here ◯◯◯◯ THAT ◯◯◯

JUMBLE®

Unscramble these four Jumbles, one letter
to each square, to form four ordinary words.

VINGY

ENDOM

FARITY

YEARTT

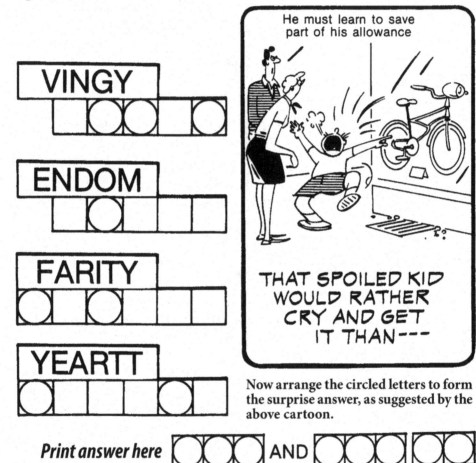

He must learn to save
part of his allowance

THAT SPOILED KID
WOULD RATHER
CRY AND GET
IT THAN---

Now arrange the circled letters to form
the surprise answer, as suggested by the
above cartoon.

Print answer here ☐☐☐ AND ☐☐☐ ☐☐

JUMBLE®

Unscramble these four Jumbles, one letter to each square, to form four ordinary words.

BITOR

MOBOL

UNGOTE

WAYELE

THEIR OLD MAN MADE MONEY IN QUESTIONABLE WAYS, AND NOW THEY'RE ENJOYING THIS.

Now arrange the circled letters to form the surprise answer, as suggested by the above cartoon.

Print answer here " ◯◯◯◯ - ◯◯◯◯◯◯◯ " GAINS

JUMBLE®

Unscramble these four Jumbles, one letter to each square, to form four ordinary words.

UNERP

DIEFT

KITSCY

SPEEXO

CUSTOMS

WHAT A SMUGGLER DOESN'T HAVE.

Now arrange the circled letters to form the surprise answer, as suggested by the above cartoon.

Print answer here A ⬭⬭⬭⬭⬭ OF ⬭⬭⬭⬭

JUMBLE

Unscramble these four Jumbles, one letter
to each square, to form four ordinary words.

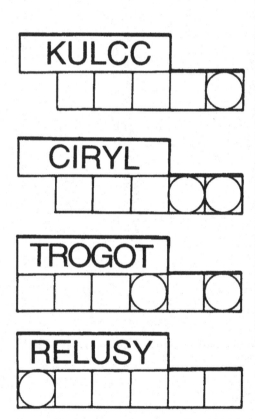

KULCC

CIRYL

TROGOT

RELUSY

What's all that noise?

THE KIND OF
WRENCH HE USED
TO LOOSEN THE
PIPE.

Now arrange the circled letters to form
the surprise answer, as suggested by the
above cartoon.

Print answer here " ☐☐☐☐ – ☐☐ "

JUMBLE®

Unscramble these four Jumbles, one letter to each square, to form four ordinary words.

WARFE

HURCS

HOPOUK

BLATOC

That one ought to fetch some real dough

WHAT THE ENTREPRENEUR ON THE HUNT WAS AFTER.

Now arrange the circled letters to form the surprise answer, as suggested by the above cartoon.

Print answer here A

JUMBLE®

Unscramble these four Jumbles, one letter
to each square, to form four ordinary words.

BOMUG

PYLAP

GLYFAD

HOGBUT

Never purchase what
you don't need

SALE

WHAT THE STU-
DENTS STUDIED
AT THE MALL.

Now arrange the circled letters to form
the surprise answer, as suggested by the
above cartoon.

Print answer here " ⬡⬡⬡ " – ⬡⬡⬡⬡⬡

JUMBLE®

Unscramble these four Jumbles, one letter
to each square, to form four ordinary words.

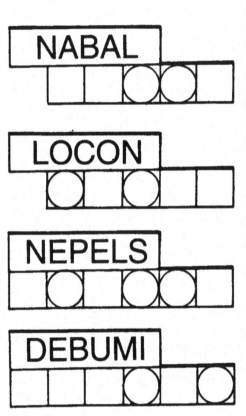

NABAL

LOCON

NEPELS

DEBUMI

Still
working?

I'm not changing
my lifestyle

WHAT DID THE
JANITOR DO WHEN
HE WON THE
LOTTERY?

Now arrange the circled letters to form
the surprise answer, as suggested by the
above cartoon.

Print answer here HE

JUMBLE®

Unscramble these four Jumbles, one letter to each square, to form four ordinary words.

GINES

RAFOL

INREET

MYSLOB

That does it!!

WHEN HIS COFFEE WAS SERVED COLD IT LEFT HIM - - -

Now arrange the circled letters to form the surprise answer, as suggested by the above cartoon.

Print answer here

57

JUMBLE®

Unscramble these four Jumbles, one letter
to each square, to form four ordinary words.

ARRIF

WARLC

GURFAL

LARROP

It makes you look younger

THE BEAUTICIAN WHO
GIVES PERMANENTS
IS CALLED THIS.

Now arrange the circled letters to form
the surprise answer, as suggested by the
above cartoon.

Print answer here A

JUMBLE®

Unscramble these four Jumbles, one letter
to each square, to form four ordinary words.

SOUPI

IXTYS

VISPLE

TROUCY

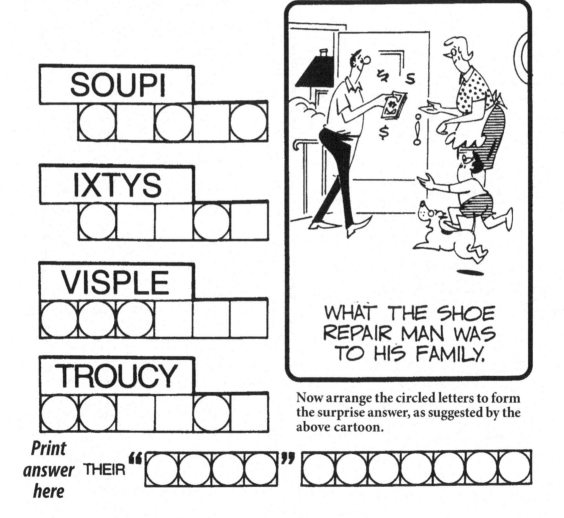

WHAT THE SHOE
REPAIR MAN WAS
TO HIS FAMILY.

Now arrange the circled letters to form
the surprise answer, as suggested by the
above cartoon.

Print
answer THEIR "⬡⬡⬡⬡⬡" ⬡⬡⬡⬡⬡⬡⬡⬡
here

JUMBLE

Unscramble these four Jumbles, one letter to each square, to form four ordinary words.

ALLAM

LIENN

BOBING

UCCSAU

It's the only one in existence

WHAT THE PRISONERS PLAYED IN THE EXERCISE YARD.

Now arrange the circled letters to form the surprise answer, as suggested by the above cartoon.

Print answer here ⬡⬡⬡ ⬡⬡⬡⬡⬡

JUMBLE®

Unscramble these four Jumbles, one letter to each square, to form four ordinary words.

CRAID

BLEER

DORFIL

NUDEAS

This is one of our most popular YAK YAK YAK

WHAT SHE WANTED THE TALKATIVE SALESLADY TO DO.

Now arrange the circled letters to form the surprise answer, as suggested by the above cartoon.

Print answer here PUT THE " ◯◯◯ " ◯◯

61

JUMBLE®

Unscramble these four Jumbles, one letter
to each square, to form four ordinary words.

TALNS

RONED

DELIJA

KUEBER

I made another
investment today

Very
risky

WHERE THE TRASH
COLLECTOR PUT
HIS MONEY.

Now arrange the circled letters to form
the surprise answer, as suggested by the
above cartoon.

Print answer here IN ⬡⬡⬡⬡ ⬡⬡⬡⬡⬡

JUMBLE®

Unscramble these four Jumbles, one letter
to each square, to form four ordinary words.

LAASI

COKAL

SHUCOR

ENGLET

BIG SALE

TO THE SHOPLIFTER
THE BELOW-COST
CLOTHING WAS THIS.

Now arrange the circled letters to form
the surprise answer, as suggested by the
above cartoon.

Print answer here A ⟨⟩⟨⟩⟨⟩⟨⟩ ⟨⟩⟨⟩⟨⟩⟨⟩⟨⟩

JUMBLE®

Unscramble these four Jumbles, one letter to each square, to form four ordinary words.

ADUCT

GOUNY

CELFIK

INJOUR

A SPORTING EVENT CAN CAUSE THIS.

Now arrange the circled letters to form the surprise answer, as suggested by the above cartoon.

Print answer here " ◯◯◯◯◯ " ◯◯◯◯

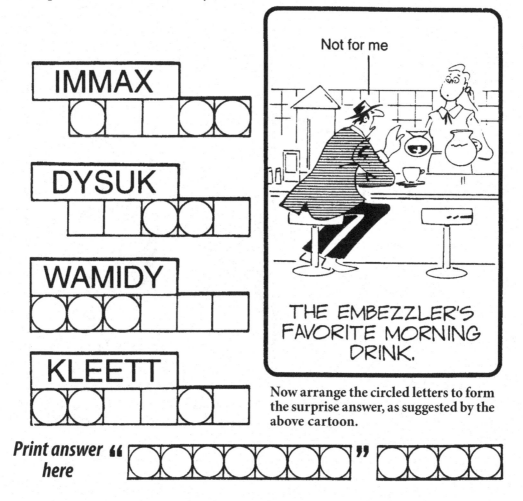

JUMBLE®

Unscramble these four Jumbles, one letter to each square, to form four ordinary words.

IMMAX

DYSUK

WAMIDY

KLEETT

Not for me

THE EMBEZZLER'S
FAVORITE MORNING
DRINK.

Now arrange the circled letters to form the surprise answer, as suggested by the above cartoon.

Print answer here " ◯◯◯◯◯◯◯ " ◯◯◯◯

JUMBLE®

Unscramble these four Jumbles, one letter
to each square, to form four ordinary words.

THIGE
◯◯◯◯◯

MATID
◯◯◯◯◯

BACHEL
◯◯◯◯◯◯

DEMPIN
◯◯◯◯◯◯

I guess he's
wet again

I used to
sleep till
nine

WHAT THEIR
BABY DID TO
THE NEW PARENTS.

Now arrange the circled letters to form
the surprise answer, as suggested by the
above cartoon.

Print answer " ◯◯◯◯◯◯◯◯ " ◯◯◯◯
here

JUMBLE®

Unscramble these four Jumbles, one letter
to each square, to form four ordinary words.

MOAXI

DUMON

ZEABAL

GATHUC

WHAT A PRIZE
FIGHTER'S DAILY
ROUTINE INCLUDES.

Now arrange the circled letters to form
the surprise answer, as suggested by the
above cartoon.

Print answer here ◯◯◯ , ◯◯◯◯◯◯

JUMBLE®

Unscramble these four Jumbles, one letter to each square, to form four ordinary words.

CABSI

CHARN

CEADAR

NECKAR

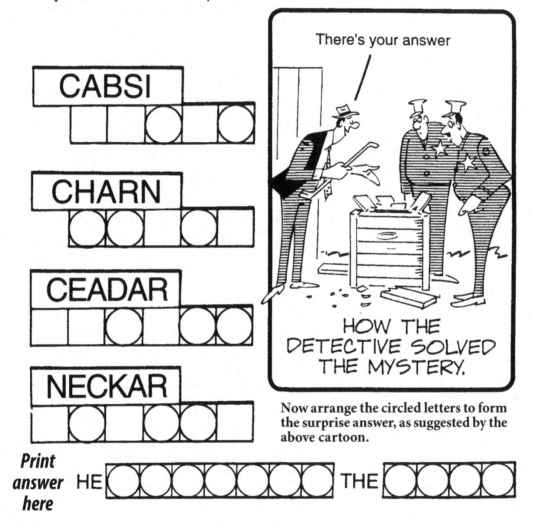

There's your answer

HOW THE
DETECTIVE SOLVED
THE MYSTERY.

Now arrange the circled letters to form the surprise answer, as suggested by the above cartoon.

Print answer here

HE ⬡⬡⬡⬡⬡⬡⬡ THE ⬡⬡⬡⬡

JUMBLE®

Unscramble these four Jumbles, one letter
to each square, to form four ordinary words.

PLUIT
◯ ◯ ◯ ◯ ◯

BUNGE
◯ ◯ ◯ ◯ ◯

ROVACT
◯ ◯ ◯ ◯ ◯ ◯

RODINO
◯ ◯ ◯ ◯ ◯ ◯

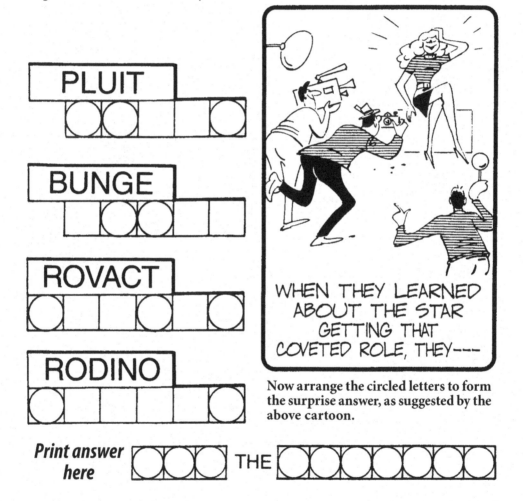

WHEN THEY LEARNED
ABOUT THE STAR
GETTING THAT
COVETED ROLE, THEY----

Now arrange the circled letters to form
the surprise answer, as suggested by the
above cartoon.

**Print answer
here** ◯◯◯ THE ◯◯◯◯◯◯◯◯

JUMBLE®

Unscramble these four Jumbles, one letter
to each square, to form four ordinary words.

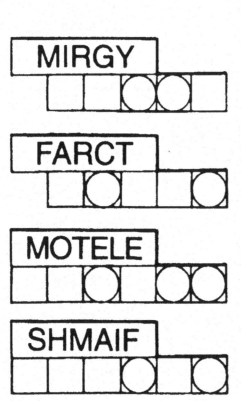

MIRGY

FARCT

MOTELE

SHMAIF

Why does she
always have to
bring me along?

WHAT SOME TAKE
WHEN THEY GO
SHOPPING.

Now arrange the circled letters to form
the surprise answer, as suggested by the
above cartoon.

Print answer here

JUMBLE®

Unscramble these four Jumbles, one letter to each square, to form four ordinary words.

MYTHE

HORAB

MUGNIP

SAHDIR

WHAT THE TALLEST PLAYER GAVE HIS COACH.

Now arrange the circled letters to form the surprise answer, as suggested by the above cartoon.

Print answer here ⬡⬡⬡⬡ ⬡⬡⬡⬡⬡

71

JUMBLE®

Unscramble these four Jumbles, one letter
to each square, to form four ordinary words.

VEROL

BERPO

KOFERD

KIELLY

Our records show
this is overdue

WHAT THE ACCOUNTANT
TURNED LIBRARIAN
REMAINED.

Now arrange the circled letters to form
the surprise answer, as suggested by the
above cartoon.

Print answer here A

JUMBLE®

Unscramble these four Jumbles, one letter to each square, to form four ordinary words.

KEEVO
[ ][ ][ ](O)(O)

PITED
[ ](O)(O)[ ]

DEDAHN
(O)[ ](O)[ ](O)[ ]

LAVASS
[ ][ ](O)(O)[ ]

SOME FOOTBALL PLAYERS
USE A PIGSKIN
TO GET THIS.

Now arrange the circled letters to form the surprise answer, as suggested by the above cartoon.

Print answer here A (O)(O)(O)(O)(O)(O)(O)(O)(O)(O)

73

JUMBLE®

Unscramble these four Jumbles, one letter to each square, to form four ordinary words.

LOGAT

STRON

CAPTER

HINCUR

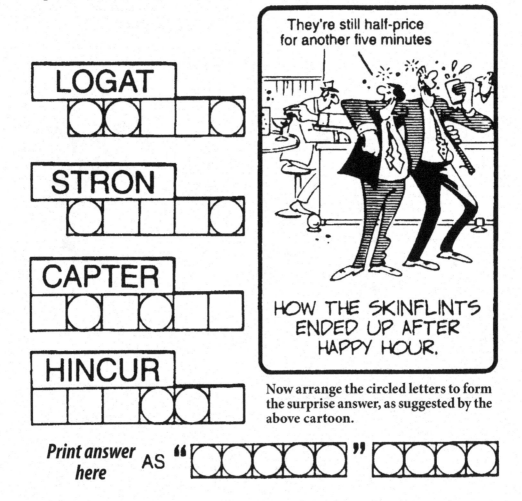

They're still half-price for another five minutes

HOW THE SKINFLINTS ENDED UP AFTER HAPPY HOUR.

Now arrange the circled letters to form the surprise answer, as suggested by the above cartoon.

Print answer here AS "☐☐☐☐☐" ☐☐☐☐

JUMBLE®

Unscramble these four Jumbles, one letter
to each square, to form four ordinary words.

ALIVA

NACYF

BOULED

CATLEK

Your check bounced

THE TIGHTROPE
WALKER GOT INTO
TROUBLE BECAUSE
HE HAD A---

Now arrange the circled letters to form
the surprise answer, as suggested by the
above cartoon.

Print answer
here ◯◯◯◯ OF ◯◯◯◯◯◯◯

JUMBLE®

Unscramble these four Jumbles, one letter to each square, to form four ordinary words.

WADAR

NERTY

NACINE

TANEBE

Good morning, Officer

WHAT THE SINGER FOUND WHEN HE BECAME A COP.

Now arrange the circled letters to form the surprise answer, as suggested by the above cartoon.

Print answer here A ⬡⬡⬡ ⬡⬡⬡⬡

JUMBLE®

Unscramble these four Jumbles, one letter to each square, to form four ordinary words.

RIMON

SEUDO

RHODIA

HYSERR

WHAT THE JANITOR
ALWAYS KEPT AT
ARM'S LENGTH.

Now arrange the circled letters to form the surprise answer, as suggested by the above cartoon.

Print answer here

JUMBLE®

Unscramble these four Jumbles, one letter
to each square, to form four ordinary words.

CHARP
◯ ◻ ◻ ◻ ◯

PERAP
◯ ◻ ◯ ◻

LOUHRY
◯ ◻ ◯ ◻ ◻ ◯

SACULE
◻ ◻ ◻ ◯ ◯ ◻

Doesn't he ever bark?

HOW SHE DESCRIBED
HER WELL-BEHAVED
YOUNG DOG.

Now arrange the circled letters to form
the surprise answer, as suggested by the
above cartoon.

Print answer here **A** ◯◯◯◯ ◯◯◯◯◯

JUMBLE®

Unscramble these four Jumbles, one letter
to each square, to form four ordinary words.

WYLEN

KOSMY

VACTAR

TUGIRA

They're everywhere

WHAT THEY BECAME
WHEN THE INSECTS
ATTACKED.

Now arrange the circled letters to form
the surprise answer, as suggested by the
above cartoon.

Print answer here THE

JUMBLE®

Unscramble these four Jumbles, one letter
to each square, to form four ordinary words.

HAGUL

TOOFA

RICCAT

HAPNOR

This stock will triple
in six months

Where have
I heard
that before?

WHAT CAN
BE FOUND IN
A SAUNA.

Now arrange the circled letters to form
the surprise answer, as suggested by the
above cartoon.

Print answer here A ☐☐☐ OF ☐☐☐ ☐☐☐

JUMBLE®

Unscramble these four Jumbles, one letter
to each square, to form four ordinary words.

CAZER

GUSET

BOYTAN

LUDGEE

Sorry for
the delay

You're always
late!

WHAT THE
PILOT RAN INTO
WHEN THE FLIGHT
WAS LATE.

Now arrange the circled letters to form
the surprise answer, as suggested by the
above cartoon.

Print answer here

JUMBLE®

Unscramble these four Jumbles, one letter to each square, to form four ordinary words.

LAUDT

TAFUL

EMSIDE

PELETS

That really makes a difference

A FACELIFT
THAT DOESN'T
COST A PENNY.

Now arrange the circled letters to form the surprise answer, as suggested by the above cartoon.

Print answer here

JUMBLE®

Unscramble these four Jumbles, one letter to each square, to form four ordinary words.

MUDIH

LAKEN

CRUNHI

FRADEO

This is impossible!

I thought this would be a nice scenic route.

THE TRAIL THROUGH THE SWAMP CAUSED THE CROSS-COUNTRY RACE TO ----

Now arrange the circled letters to form the surprise answer, as suggested by the above cartoon.

Print answer here ⬜⬜⬜ " ⬜ - ⬜⬜⬜⬜ "

JUMBLE®

Unscramble these four Jumbles, one letter to each square, to form four ordinary words.

REAPO

PNTES

SOOPEP

CURPSE

Call it in the air.

Heads! No, tails! No, wait, I mean heads.

WHETHER OR NOT THE COIN WOULD LAND HEADS OR TAILS WAS ---

Now arrange the circled letters to form the surprise answer, as suggested by the above cartoon.

Print answer here A

JUMBLE®

Unscramble these four Jumbles, one letter to each square, to form four ordinary words.

PYRCT

DALMY

DEEMLY

PAPREA

You look great in them. They are half off today.

They're perfect. And perfect for my budget.

1/2 Off SALE!

SHE THOUGHT THE NEW GLASSES WERE ---

Now arrange the circled letters to form the surprise answer, as suggested by the above cartoon.

Print answer here " ◯◯◯ - ◯◯◯◯ "

85

JUMBLE®

Unscramble these four Jumbles, one letter to each square, to form four ordinary words.

SHAYT

UNDEC

METLUB

WYSLAA

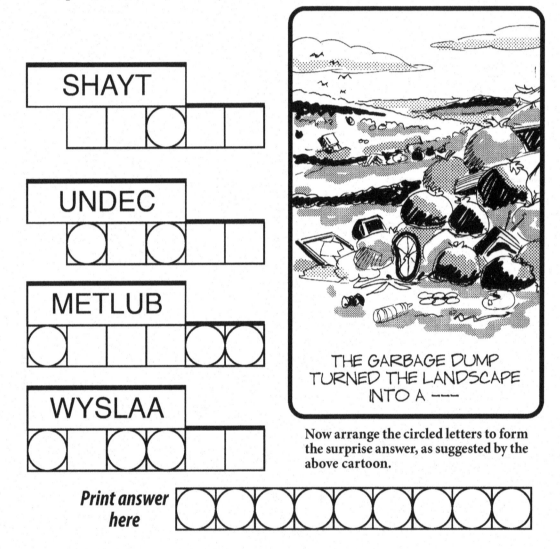

THE GARBAGE DUMP TURNED THE LANDSCAPE INTO A ---

Now arrange the circled letters to form the surprise answer, as suggested by the above cartoon.

Print answer here

JUMBLE®

Unscramble these four Jumbles, one letter
to each square, to form four ordinary words.

KUYYC

BEAID

RUGHYN

CLORSL

These shrubs
are overgrown.

They've really
taken off.

THE SHRUBS NEEDED
TRIMMING BECAUSE THEY
WERE TOO ----

Now arrange the circled letters to form
the surprise answer, as suggested by the
above cartoon.

Print answer here

JUMBLE®

Unscramble these four Jumbles, one letter
to each square, to form four ordinary words.

NILFT

TRUBS

SLEIYA

PEOOSP

I like the
seclusion.

I just
love it out
here.

CASPER BOUGHT A CABIN IN
THE WOODS SO THAT HE
COULD LIVE IN THE ----

Now arrange the circled letters to form
the surprise answer, as suggested by the
above cartoon.

Print answer here "◯◯◯-◯◯◯◯"

JUMBLE®

Unscramble these four Jumbles, one letter to each square, to form four ordinary words.

TAUQO

TENIW

SODWIN

LUFOND

OUT OF BUSINESS

Have these been sold?

Yep. A grocery store bought them.

WHEN THE BOTTLED WATER COMPANY WENT BANKRUPT, ITS STOCK WAS ----

Now arrange the circled letters to form the surprise answer, as suggested by the above cartoon.

Print answer here

JUMBLE®

Unscramble these four Jumbles, one letter to each square, to form four ordinary words.

DIGRI

FADUR

SIHINF

TAREYE

Down in front!

KING KONG ATTENDED YANKEES GAMES BECAUSE HE WAS A ---

Now arrange the circled letters to form the surprise answer, as suggested by the above cartoon.

Print answer here

JUMBLE®

Unscramble these four Jumbles, one letter to each square, to form four ordinary words.

VOIDE

LIBND

GENLIM

AIRSOL

So, how was your day?

It was busy. We had four funerals. I'm glad to be home.

AFTER WORKING ALL DAY AT THE FUNERAL HOME, HE WAS HAPPY TO GET BACK TO HIS ---

Now arrange the circled letters to form the surprise answer, as suggested by the above cartoon.

Print answer here

JUMBLE®

Unscramble these four Jumbles, one letter to each square, to form four ordinary words.

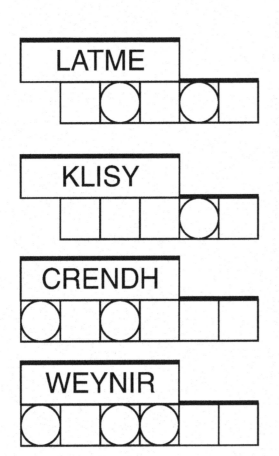

LATME

KLISY

CRENDH

WEYNIR

Are you OK? You've been falling behind.

I think I'd better head home and crawl into bed.

AFTER GETTING SICK FRIDAY, ON SATURDAY, SHE WAS ———

Now arrange the circled letters to form the surprise answer, as suggested by the above cartoon.

Print answer here ⬡⬡⬡⬡⬡⬡⬡⬡

JUMBLE®

Unscramble these four Jumbles, one letter to each square, to form four ordinary words.

PARGH

TIKYT

TUMCOS

GUNFEL

To no one's surprise, Blabber Inc. declares bankruptcy.

I heard he put his clients into that company.

BLABBER INC.

Oh, no!

BLABBER INC.

AFTER BUYING SHARES IN A COMPANY THAT WENT BANKRUPT THE NEXT DAY, THE BROKER WAS A ----

Now arrange the circled letters to form the surprise answer, as suggested by the above cartoon.

Print answer here

93

JUMBLE®

Unscramble these four Jumbles, one letter to each square, to form four ordinary words.

GALIE

POLEE

HAWYON

RUYSPY

This is going to be a huge problem. We can't do that instantly.

You're going to have to clear this whole floor, ASAP.

WHEN THE KING NEEDED TO GO TO THE HOSPITAL, IT WAS A ---

Now arrange the circled letters to form the surprise answer, as suggested by the above cartoon.

Print answer here

JUMBLE®

Unscramble these four Jumbles, one letter to each square, to form four ordinary words.

HOUCC

RUBYL

GEALEL

SICBET

Get out of here!

Where do they all come from?

THEIR BREAKFAST BY THE WATER INCLUDED ---

Now arrange the circled letters to form the surprise answer, as suggested by the above cartoon.

Print answer here

95

JUMBLE®

Unscramble these four Jumbles, one letter
to each square, to form four ordinary words.

TUCEA

SKPYE

ADEZMA

PPORRE

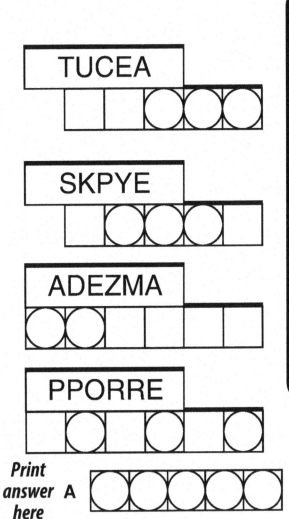

meat

bakery

produce

This new
store is
terrific!

Wow!
Fresh
baguettes.

THE SHOPPERS THOUGHT
THE NEW GROCERY
STORE WAS ----

Now arrange the circled letters to form
the surprise answer, as suggested by the
above cartoon.

Print
answer **A**
here

96

JUMBLE®

Unscramble these four Jumbles, one letter
to each square, to form four ordinary words.

DEZDA

GALEE

DUNROG

DIHNED

What great
defense!

THE NIGHT WATCHMAN,
VIEWING THE BASKETBALL
GAME ON TV, PARTICULARLY
LIKED ALL THE ----

Now arrange the circled letters to form
the surprise answer, as suggested by the
above cartoon.

Print answer here

JUMBLE®

Unscramble these four Jumbles, one letter
to each square, to form four ordinary words.

MOAAR

PNIRT

CEDEDO

LONPEL

Here you go.
You get what
you pay for.
And it's the
best.

It looks
great up
there.

TO GET THEIR FANCY
NEW CHURCH SPIRE,
THEY ---

Now arrange the circled letters to form
the surprise answer, as suggested by the
above cartoon.

**Print
answer
here**

JUMBLE®

Unscramble these four Jumbles, one letter
to each square, to form four ordinary words.

DARFU

KAYLE

VISLEW

MABCEE

Boca Vista Bridge
Tournament

Well, I thought
I had those
ten tricks.

Well, you didn't.
Now we're
going home
losers.

Uh, bye,
guys.

AFTER LOSING THE
GAME, THE BRIDGE
PARTNERS ---

Now arrange the circled letters to form
the surprise answer, as suggested by the
above cartoon.

**Print
answer
here**

JUMBLE®

Unscramble these four Jumbles, one letter to each square, to form four ordinary words.

PRICH

BOREP

TURMET

REUSAS

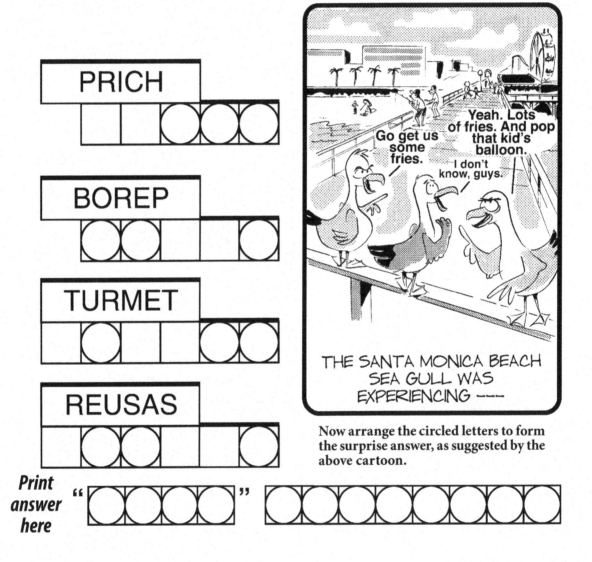

Go get us some fries.

Yeah. Lots of fries. And pop that kid's balloon.

I don't know, guys.

THE SANTA MONICA BEACH SEA GULL WAS EXPERIENCING ---

Now arrange the circled letters to form the surprise answer, as suggested by the above cartoon.

Print answer here " ☐☐☐☐ " ☐☐☐☐☐☐☐☐

100

JUMBLE®

Unscramble these four Jumbles, one letter
to each square, to form four ordinary words.

SOJUT

CASEE

SCACES

ROCXAB

What went wrong
out there?

Nothing.
He got
lucky.
Get me
an ice
pack.

HE DIDN'T WANT TO TALK
ABOUT HIS WRESTLING
MATCH LOSS BECAUSE IT
WAS A ---

Now arrange the circled letters to form
the surprise answer, as suggested by the
above cartoon.

*Print
answer
here*

JUMBLE®

Unscramble these four Jumbles, one letter
to each square, to form four ordinary words.

WALBY

LATYL

FRADYT

ZERFYN

Well, aren't
they
special.

Steep Up Cafe

Serving
Earl Grey
Black
Green
White
Matcha

WHEN SHE SAW THE FANCY
NEW CAFÉ THAT SERVED
EARL GREY AND CHAI, SHE
THOUGHT ----

Now arrange the circled letters to form
the surprise answer, as suggested by the
above cartoon.

Print answer here "◯◯ - ◯◯◯ - ◯◯"

PUZZLE 101

JUMBLE®

Unscramble these four Jumbles, one letter to each square, to form four ordinary words.

SERDS

FUNTI

DREEEG

BARBOS

Now, what if I can't sleep on this?
I promise you'll sleep like a baby.
SLEEP SALE!
BOB

HE ASKED IF THE MATTRESS CAME WITH A WARRANTY, AND THE SALESMAN TOLD HIM HE COULD ---

Now arrange the circled letters to form the surprise answer, as suggested by the above cartoon.

Print answer here

JUMBLE®

Unscramble these four Jumbles, one letter to each square, to form four ordinary words.

GINTE

OCIVE

PAAREP

SOWDAH

Are you kidding me? We can actually defend ourselves with these!

I just think stones are better.

HE POKED HIS SKEPTICAL BUDDY WITH THE NEW SPEAR TO ---

Now arrange the circled letters to form the surprise answer, as suggested by the above cartoon.

Print answer here

JUMBLE®

Unscramble these four Jumbles, one letter to each square, to form four ordinary words.

BAROH

LGIRL

LEANHI

TOSUMT

I need them to get back to work.

WHEN THE MACHINERY AT THE LUMBER FACTORY BROKE DOWN, EVERYONE WAS ---

Now arrange the circled letters to form the surprise answer, as suggested by the above cartoon.

Print answer here

JUMBLE®

Unscramble these four Jumbles, one letter to each square, to form four ordinary words.

SHOTI

HGEED

KREMTA

SUFEED

Whoa!
Don't tackle
me.

AFTER THROWING THE
TOUCHDOWN PASS
TO WIN THE GAME, HIS
TEAMMATES ---

Now arrange the circled letters to form the surprise answer, as suggested by the above cartoon.

Print answer here

JUMBLE®

Unscramble these four Jumbles, one letter
to each square, to form four ordinary words.

CADYE

SRIBK

SNARTD

TANWED

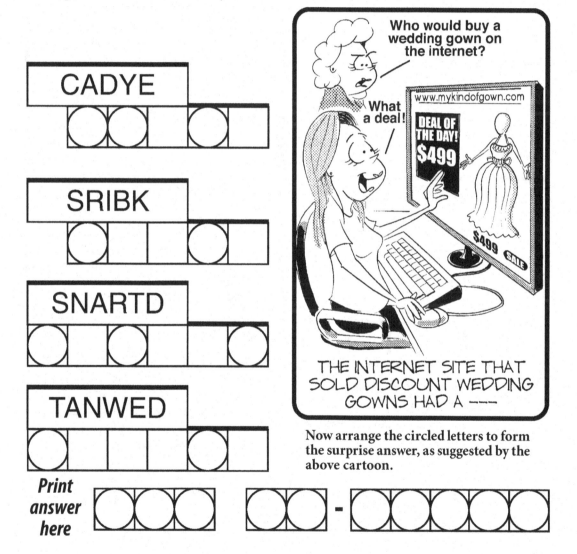

Who would buy a
wedding gown on
the internet?

What
a deal!

www.mykindofgown.com

DEAL OF
THE DAY!
$499

$499 SALE

THE INTERNET SITE THAT
SOLD DISCOUNT WEDDING
GOWNS HAD A ---

Now arrange the circled letters to form
the surprise answer, as suggested by the
above cartoon.

Print
answer
here

⎕⎕⎕ ⎕⎕ - ⎕⎕⎕⎕⎕

JUMBLE®

Unscramble these four Jumbles, one letter to each square, to form four ordinary words.

CIMMI

DEAGA

SWOORR

TERPYO

Looks like you've got a charley horse.

Ow! I need to stretch.

WHEN THE AUTHOR WENT FOR A HORSEBACK RIDE, HE ENDED UP GETTING ----

Now arrange the circled letters to form the surprise answer, as suggested by the above cartoon.

Print answer here " ◯◯◯◯◯ ' ◯ " ◯◯◯◯◯◯

JUMBLE®

Unscramble these four Jumbles, one letter to each square, to form four ordinary words.

CEKEH

ZAAME

MADREY

SPOPEO

AFTER THE
PIT STOP,
THE RACE CAR ---

Now arrange the circled letters to form the surprise answer, as suggested by the above cartoon.

Print answer here ◯◯ - ◯◯◯◯◯◯◯

JUMBLE®

Unscramble these four Jumbles, one letter
to each square, to form four ordinary words.

KINYD

USISE

RIVNET

TOFERF

What do you guys
want to do now?

I don't care.
Whatever.

Doesn't
matter to me.

THE IDENTICAL TWINS WERE
JUST ALIKE, EVEN WHEN
THEY WERE ----

Now arrange the circled letters to form
the surprise answer, as suggested by the
above cartoon.

Print
answer
here

JUMBLE®

Unscramble these four Jumbles, one letter to each square, to form four ordinary words.

DREDU

ANTUT

CRUONK

CUQLIE

I am next in line for the crown, you twit!

That doeseth it! Let us goeth!

WHEN THE BRITISH NOBLEMEN GOT INTO AN ARGUMENT, THEY ---

Now arrange the circled letters to form the surprise answer, as suggested by the above cartoon.

Print answer here

111

JUMBLE®

Unscramble these four Jumbles, one letter
to each square, to form four ordinary words.

STNEP

BROTO

VICTEA

MACYLM

What is this? I can drink this in one sip!

That's the way we serve them. I shook it, just like you asked.

JAMES BOND COMPLAINED
ABOUT HIS DRINK BECAUSE
IT WAS TOO ----

Now arrange the circled letters to form
the surprise answer, as suggested by the
above cartoon.

Print answer here " ◯◯◯ - ◯◯◯◯◯ "

JUMBLE®

Unscramble these four Jumbles, one letter to each square, to form four ordinary words.

MIPLE

ALKIE

GUCTAH

TINYTE

Great job tonight! I think we all need some rest.

We make a great team.

AFTER HUNTING ALL NIGHT, THE WOLVES DECIDED TO ---

Now arrange the circled letters to form the surprise answer, as suggested by the above cartoon.

Print answer here

113

JUMBLE®

Unscramble these four Jumbles, one letter to each square, to form four ordinary words.

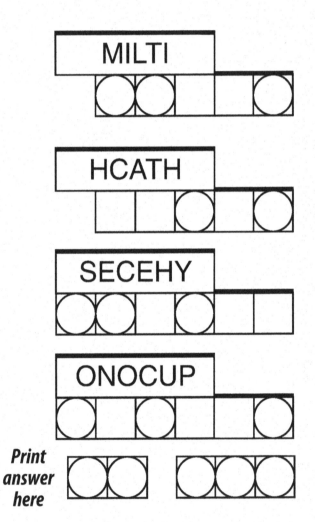

MILTI

HCATH

SECEHY

ONOCUP

Print answer here

Wow! You really came through. Now, we can get to the theater on time.

It's shifting smoothly now.

THE TRANSMISSION MECHANIC CAME THROUGH ---

Now arrange the circled letters to form the surprise answer, as suggested by the above cartoon.

114

JUMBLE®

Unscramble these four Jumbles, one letter to each square, to form four ordinary words.

LANMY

DLEWL

TANTFE

DIRIBE

This stuff is really good.

This is fun!

WHEN THE SCARECROWS HAD AN OUTING, THEY HAD A ---

Now arrange the circled letters to form the surprise answer, as suggested by the above cartoon.

Print answer here

JUMBLE®

Unscramble these four Jumbles, one letter
to each square, to form four ordinary words.

CASHO

HHSAR

CRAYIP

LEHTEM

GONNA GETCHA!
Best Bounty
Hunting

I need to
trademark that
saying.

I can hear
people
saying that
right now.

THE BOUNTY HUNTER'S
SLOGAN WAS A ----

Now arrange the circled letters to form
the surprise answer, as suggested by the
above cartoon.

Print
answer
here

JUMBLE®

Unscramble these four Jumbles, one letter
to each square, to form four ordinary words.

CINEM

PARHG

GIRNTS

CNECTA

It's a good thing you ordered these months ago.

That's why I'm the best wedding planner around.

WHEN A LOT OF BOUQUETS WERE NEEDED, THEY MADE ----

Now arrange the circled letters to form
the surprise answer, as suggested by the
above cartoon.

Print
answer
here

JUMBLE®

Unscramble these four Jumbles, one letter
to each square, to form four ordinary words.

WELYN

BIRTO

CIJNET

LUDONF

Why doesn't this sound right?

That's the old score. Didn't you get the email last night?

THE CONCERT MUSIC
WAS CHANGED, BUT THE
MUSICIAN HADN'T BEEN ----

Now arrange the circled letters to form
the surprise answer, as suggested by the
above cartoon.

Print answer " ☐☐☐☐☐ - ☐☐☐☐☐☐ "
here

JUMBLE®

Unscramble these four Jumbles, one letter
to each square, to form four ordinary words.

LUGEN

AHCOV

DOUPIM

TEPICO

Look how strong he is.

It's like that car is a toy. This is awesome.

AUDIENCES LOVED "JURASSIC PARK" AND THOUGHT IT WAS ----

Now arrange the circled letters to form
the surprise answer, as suggested by the
above cartoon.

Print answer " ⬡⬡⬡⬡ - ⬡⬡⬡⬡⬡ "
here

JUMBLE®

Unscramble these four Jumbles, one letter to each square, to form four ordinary words.

MAHES

CEWIT

NEDORT

HEYCAP

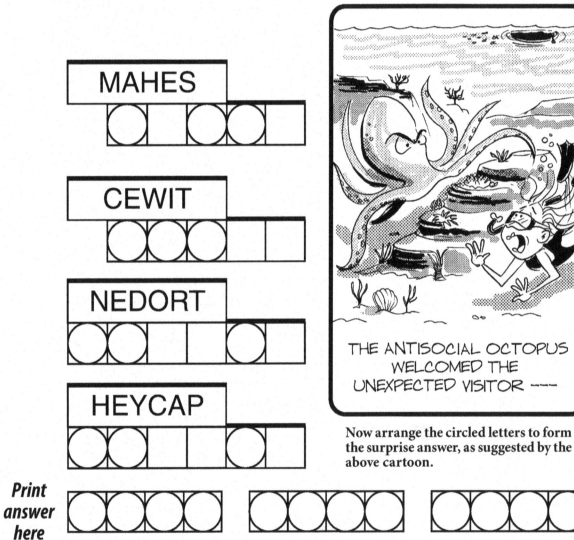

THE ANTISOCIAL OCTOPUS
WELCOMED THE
UNEXPECTED VISITOR ----

Now arrange the circled letters to form the surprise answer, as suggested by the above cartoon.

Print
answer
here

JUMBLE®

Unscramble these four Jumbles, one letter
to each square, to form four ordinary words.

CUYYK

DARYT

TAXFIE

BRASUD

It's been
a busy
year.

We have
reorders
for the
Grumpy
Cat.

I'm just
going to
solve all
366
Jumble
puzzles.

THE CALENDAR FACTORY
PRODUCED
CALENDARS ---

Now arrange the circled letters to form
the surprise answer, as suggested by the
above cartoon.

Print
answer
here

JUMBLE®

Unscramble these four Jumbles, one letter to each square, to form four ordinary words.

LIHYL

RUCYR

AMDTEN

GAULEE

I like how the symbol is easy to write.

It has no beginning or end, so it could also stand for infinity.

4+4=8

THE NUMBER THAT EQUALS FOUR PLUS FOUR DIDN'T EXIST UNTIL IT WAS ———

Now arrange the circled letters to form the surprise answer, as suggested by the above cartoon.

Print answer here " ◯◯◯ - ◯◯◯◯◯ - ◯◯ "

JUMBLE®

Unscramble these four Jumbles, one letter to each square, to form four ordinary words.

TAHEW

NIRKB

CLEANC

GRIBTH

So, what's two times two?

2X1=
2X2=
2X3=
2X4=
2X5=

That's easy. Four!

SHE KNEW WHAT TWO TIMES TWO EQUALED AND DIDN'T HAVE TO ---

Now arrange the circled letters to form the surprise answer, as suggested by the above cartoon.

Print answer here

JUMBLE®

Unscramble these four Jumbles, one letter
to each square, to form four ordinary words.

UNDOW

DIGYD

GIMSAT

PICANT

Isn't it great? They took
your old one for free.

What did you do?
I want my chair
back!

SHE THREW OUT HIS OLD
RECLINER AND HE WASN'T
GOING TO TAKE IT ---

Now arrange the circled letters to form
the surprise answer, as suggested by the
above cartoon.

Print
answer
here

JUMBLE®

Unscramble these four Jumbles, one letter to each square, to form four ordinary words.

FRAWH

NORGP

SAJTUD

SLURPA

Picture an afternoon temperature of 864 on Venus and Earth having a temp of 57.

THE ATMOSPHERES OF VENUS AND EARTH ARE ----

Now arrange the circled letters to form the surprise answer, as suggested by the above cartoon.

Print answer here

JUMBLE®

Unscramble these four Jumbles, one letter
to each square, to form four ordinary words.

PUYGP

BAINC

ROMMEY

TERATO

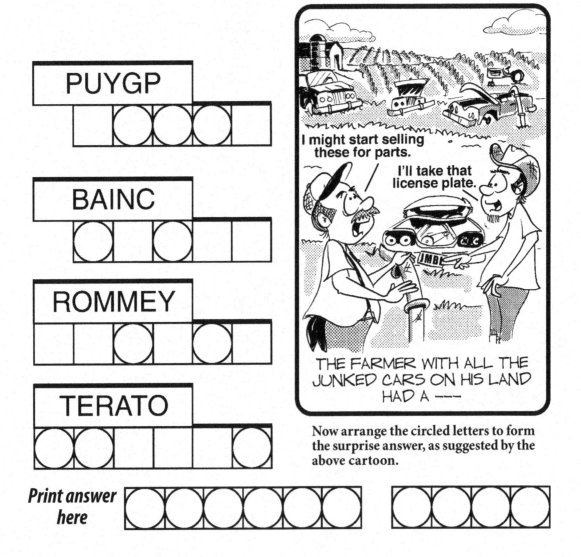

I might start selling
these for parts.

I'll take that
license plate.

THE FARMER WITH ALL THE
JUNKED CARS ON HIS LAND
HAD A ---

Now arrange the circled letters to form
the surprise answer, as suggested by the
above cartoon.

Print answer
here

JUMBLE®

Unscramble these four Jumbles, one letter to each square, to form four ordinary words.

RAWYE

DIGRI

SANXYT

GUHACT

Well, I figured out the damage. Are you ready to write the check?

Are we going to have anything left?

WHAT DOES YOUR MONEY BECOME WHEN YOU COMBINE "THE" AND "IRS"?

Now arrange the circled letters to form the surprise answer, as suggested by the above cartoon.

Print answer here

JUMBLE®

Unscramble these four Jumbles, one letter
to each square, to form four ordinary words.

NAYLM

TIDOT

SPWIRA

YOGAVE

Traffic is
horrible
today.

No room
to pass.

TRAFFIC ON
THE HORSE FARM
WAS CAUSED BY ---

Now arrange the circled letters to form
the surprise answer, as suggested by the
above cartoon.

*Print
answer
here* " ◯◯◯◯◯ - ◯◯◯◯◯◯◯ "

JUMBLE®

Unscramble these four Jumbles, one letter to each square, to form four ordinary words.

LOYID

REVAB

WLIPOL

BLOYMS

Are you going to take the kids swimming?

Look, I have a conference call and a ton of emails.

THE ALLIGATOR WAS STRESSED OUT BECAUSE HE WAS ----

Now arrange the circled letters to form the surprise answer, as suggested by the above cartoon.

Print answer here

JUMBLE®

Unscramble these four Jumbles, one letter
to each square, to form four ordinary words.

DYNHA

GOUBS

RIYVEF

DENORY

It's great
having the
old team
together.

I'm so glad
you made
it.

I couldn't
miss seeing
everyone.

Smile.

WHEN THE GROUP OF FRIENDS
TOOK A PHOTO TOGETHER,
THEY TOOK A PHOTO OF ----

Now arrange the circled letters to form
the surprise answer, as suggested by the
above cartoon.

Print
answer
here

" ⃝⃝⃝⃝⃝ - ⃝⃝⃝⃝⃝ "

JUMBLE®

Unscramble these four Jumbles, one letter
to each square, to form four ordinary words.

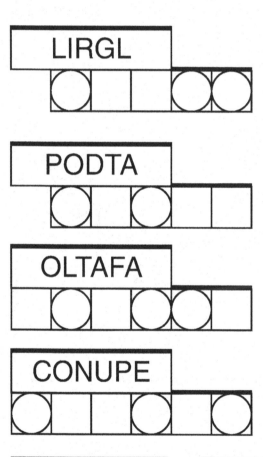

LIRGL

PODTA

OLTAFA

CONUPE

That should mark the spot.

Let me get a picture of this.

WHEN AMUNDSEN REACHED THE
BOTTOM OF THE EARTH IN 1911,
HE PUT A ─ ─ ─

Now arrange the circled letters to form
the surprise answer, as suggested by the
above cartoon.

Print answer here

131

JUMBLE®

Unscramble these four Jumbles, one letter
to each square, to form four ordinary words.

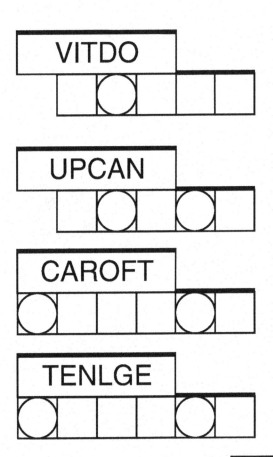

VITDO

UPCAN

CAROFT

TENLGE

Why aren't you working? What are we paying you for!

I'm taste-testing

NEW AT THE BREAD COMPANY, HE WAS OFTEN CAUGHT ----

Now arrange the circled letters to form the surprise answer, as suggested by the above cartoon.

Print answer here

JUMBLE®

Unscramble these four Jumbles, one letter
to each square, to form four ordinary words.

CINCY

LEPSL

GRULAF

TIEPOT

THERE ARE MORE THAN
1,000 SATELLITES ORBITING
EARTH, BECAUSE THERE'S ----

There
she
goes.

There's
plenty of
room for it.

Now arrange the circled letters to form
the surprise answer, as suggested by the
above cartoon.

*Print
answer
here*

JUMBLE®

Unscramble these four Jumbles, one letter
to each square, to form four ordinary words.

COSAH

CLEET

ROSWOR

OYMENK

How did they
do that without
thumbs?

Wow!

WHEN THE RANCHER'S
CATTLE ESCAPED UNDER
THE FENCE, HE SAID ---

Now arrange the circled letters to form
the surprise answer, as suggested by the
above cartoon.

Print answer " ◯◯◯◯-◯ " ◯◯◯
here

JUMBLE®

Unscramble these four Jumbles, one letter
to each square, to form four ordinary words.

CANTE

BIRTO

DAPCMA

RUXULY

This is our
new favorite
place.

How's
business?

I've had a full
house
every night.

WITH EACH GLASS OF
WINE THEY FILLED,
MONEY ----

Now arrange the circled letters to form
the surprise answer, as suggested by the
above cartoon.

Print answer here

JUMBLE®

Unscramble these four Jumbles, one letter to each square, to form four ordinary words.

GAMIE

RAHHS

REPPOR

CRANEP

Mom said something like, "Come when you're ready."

I believe she said, "Be home on time."

WHEN THE TWINS SPOKE AT THE SAME TIME, SOMETIMES THEY WOULD ---

Now arrange the circled letters to form the surprise answer, as suggested by the above cartoon.

Print answer here

" ☐☐☐☐ - ☐ - ☐☐☐☐☐☐☐ "

JUMBLE®

Unscramble these four Jumbles, one letter to each square, to form four ordinary words.

COLAV

GINET

MIRNOF

BIRCES

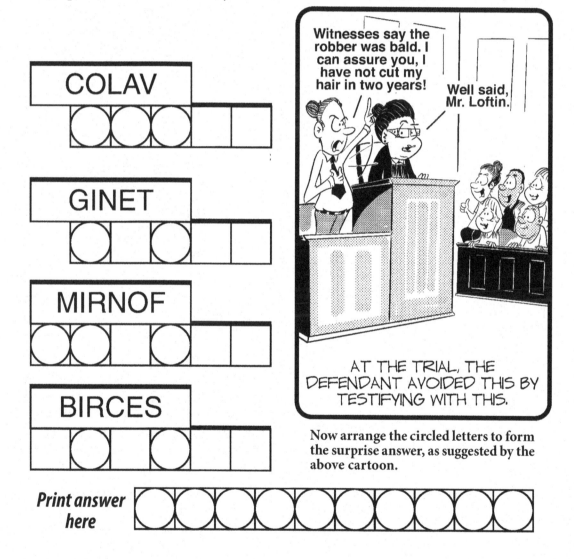

Witnesses say the robber was bald. I can assure you, I have not cut my hair in two years!

Well said, Mr. Loftin.

AT THE TRIAL, THE DEFENDANT AVOIDED THIS BY TESTIFYING WITH THIS.

Now arrange the circled letters to form the surprise answer, as suggested by the above cartoon.

Print answer here

JUMBLE®

Unscramble these four Jumbles, one letter
to each square, to form four ordinary words.

LIDUF

LOFDO

RODTIR

ZHRAAD

I'll be able
to bring
taxes
down to
zero
percent!

I'll make
everyone in
the country a
millionaire!

We're
going
too
high!

WHEN THE POLITICIANS WENT
FOR A BALLOON RIDE, THE
BALLOON WAS ---

Now arrange the circled letters to form
the surprise answer, as suggested by the
above cartoon.

Print
answer
here

138

JUMBLE®

Unscramble these four Jumbles, one letter
to each square, to form four ordinary words.

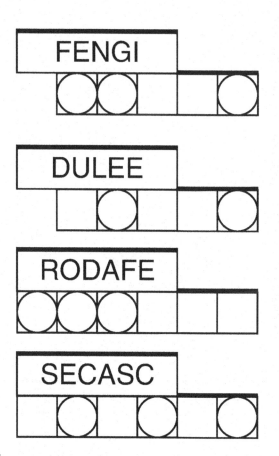

FENGI

DULEE

RODAFE

SECASC

Don's Dojo

Why didn't you
hire someone
to put this up?

I can
protect
myself.

THE KARATE INSTRUCTOR
INSTALLED HIS OWN WROUGHT
IRON BECAUSE HE WANTED ----

Now arrange the circled letters to form
the surprise answer, as suggested by the
above cartoon.

*Print
answer
here*

" ◯◯ - ◯◯◯◯◯ "

JUMBLE®

Unscramble these four Jumbles, one letter
to each square, to form four ordinary words.

DAHYN

VLIAA

PGRINS

ROLLFA

Yum!
She's
good!

I hope she can
cook this way
every night.

THEY HOPED THE CHEF
WOULD BE A LONG-TERM
HIT, NOT JUST A ----

Now arrange the circled letters to form
the surprise answer, as suggested by the
above cartoon.

*Print
answer
here*

THE

140

JUMBLE®

Unscramble these four Jumbles, one letter to each square, to form four ordinary words.

VRYAG

UTINP

BUREPS

PANHEP

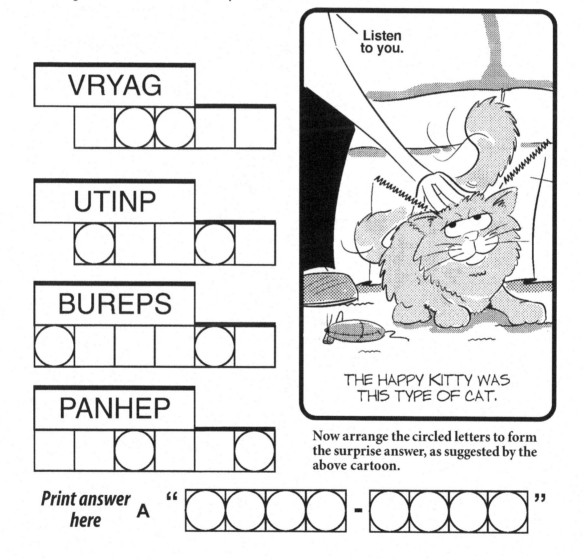

Listen to you.

THE HAPPY KITTY WAS THIS TYPE OF CAT.

Now arrange the circled letters to form the surprise answer, as suggested by the above cartoon.

Print answer here A " ◯◯◯◯ - ◯◯◯◯ "

141

JUMBLE®

Unscramble these four Jumbles, one letter to each square, to form four ordinary words.

FITUN

THINN

WALHIE

SOLYGS

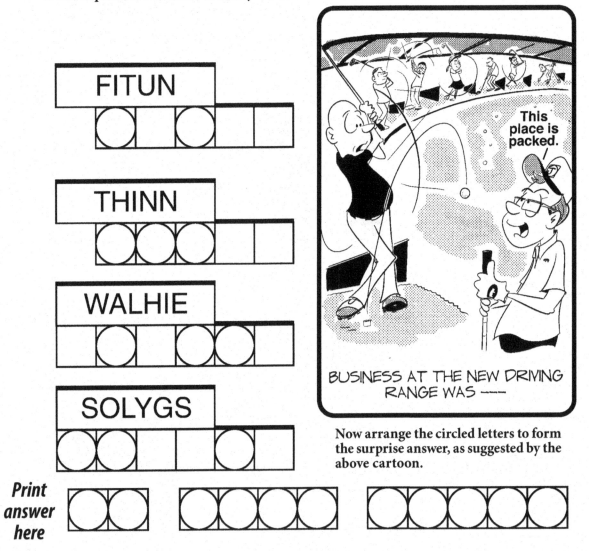

This place is packed.

BUSINESS AT THE NEW DRIVING RANGE WAS ----

Now arrange the circled letters to form the surprise answer, as suggested by the above cartoon.

Print answer here

JUMBLE®

Unscramble these four Jumbles, one letter to each square, to form four ordinary words.

RAYWE

MUDIH

CHLIGT

TUNBOY

DARRIN STEPHENS WAS INSTANTLY ATTRACTED TO SAMANTHA AND FOUND HER ----

Now arrange the circled letters to form the surprise answer, as suggested by the above cartoon.

Print answer here

JUMBLE®

Unscramble these four Jumbles, one letter to each square, to form four ordinary words.

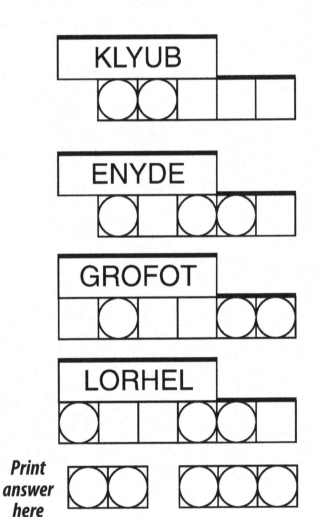

KLYUB

ENYDE

GROFOT

LORHEL

Wow! He really turned it on after rounding first base.

HE HURRIED TO SECOND BASE BECAUSE HE WANTED TO GET THERE ---

Now arrange the circled letters to form the surprise answer, as suggested by the above cartoon.

Print answer here

144

JUMBLE®

Unscramble these four Jumbles, one letter to each square, to form four ordinary words.

CELUN

LEABC

DINSIG

TONKYT

I've wanted to do this my whole life.

He keeps trying new things.

I hope he survives.

Are you ready, cowboy?

HE RODE THE MECHANICAL BULL BECAUSE IT WAS ON HIS ---

Now arrange the circled letters to form the surprise answer, as suggested by the above cartoon.

Print answer here " ⬭⬭⬭⬭ - ⬭⬭ " ⬭⬭⬭⬭

JUMBLE®

Unscramble these four Jumbles, one letter to each square, to form four ordinary words.

WNLOF

LOYHL

CATJEK

TANTIA

Thank you! Good night!

I really like her plans.

I can't wait to tell my club about this.

This will make a great article.

WHEN THE MAYOR GAVE HER ANNUAL SPEECH, IT WAS THE ---

Now arrange the circled letters to form the surprise answer, as suggested by the above cartoon.

Print answer here

146

JUMBLE®

Unscramble these four Jumbles, one letter to each square, to form four ordinary words.

ERVAB

USDOK

CENTHS

YETLIV

Your grades are great. Why doubt yourself?

I don't know. Maybe I should go in a different direction.

Honey, you've chosen the right path. Trust us.

SHE WANTED TO DROP SCIENCE, BUT HER PARENTS ADVISED HER TO – – –

Now arrange the circled letters to form the surprise answer, as suggested by the above cartoon.

Print answer here

☐☐☐☐ ☐☐☐ ☐☐☐☐☐☐☐

JUMBLE®

Unscramble these four Jumbles, one letter to each square, to form four ordinary words.

TNHIN

NEPDU

TAFALO

DLIFED

You'll have to do better than that next time, Hook!

I'll get you yet!

CAPTAIN HOOK WANTED TO CAPTURE PETER AND THE LOST BOYS, BUT HIS PLANS ----

Now arrange the circled letters to form the surprise answer, as suggested by the above cartoon.

Print answer here

JUMBLE®

Unscramble these four Jumbles, one letter
to each square, to form four ordinary words.

CNIPH

SMAHE

VIEIDD

MARUAT

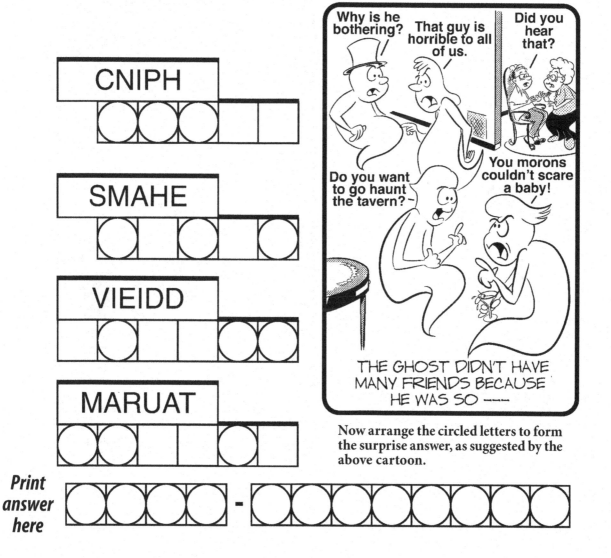

Why is he bothering?

That guy is horrible to all of us.

Did you hear that?

Do you want to go haunt the tavern?

You morons couldn't scare a baby!

THE GHOST DIDN'T HAVE
MANY FRIENDS BECAUSE
HE WAS SO ----

Now arrange the circled letters to form
the surprise answer, as suggested by the
above cartoon.

Print
answer
here

◯◯◯◯◯ - ◯◯◯◯◯◯◯◯◯◯

JUMBLE®

Unscramble these four Jumbles, one letter to each square, to form four ordinary words.

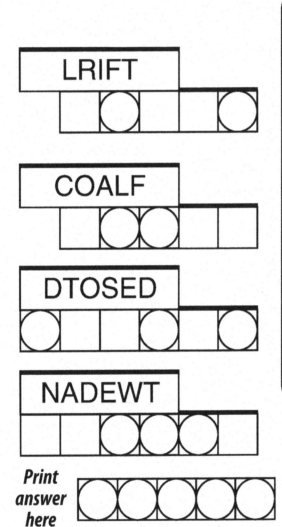

LRIFT

COALF

DTOSED

NADEWT

Aren't you voting?

Nah. I'm training today.

Why would you abstain?

VOTING ALLOWS YOU TO MAKE YOUR VOICE HEARD, UNLESS YOU ----

Now arrange the circled letters to form the surprise answer, as suggested by the above cartoon.

Print answer here

PUZZLE
149

JUMBLE®

Unscramble these four Jumbles, one letter
to each square, to form four ordinary words.

KAHYS

PUTRE

NITRGS

LOGONB

Lads, I will not
tolerate yelling and
playing ball in the
hallways.

THE YOUNG MEN RUNNING
INDOORS WERE DISCIPLINED
FOR BEING TOO ----

Now arrange the circled letters to form
the surprise answer, as suggested by the
above cartoon.

Print
answer
here "◯◯◯ - ◯◯◯◯◯◯◯"

JUMBLE®

Unscramble these four Jumbles, one letter to each square, to form four ordinary words.

LAZWT

NEAAR

YEDDAB

SOMSCO

I can't believe how full those nets are.

Forrest, we should open a restaurant with all the money we're hauling in.

WHEN IT CAME TO MONEY, THE SUCCESSFUL SHRIMP COMPANY ----

Now arrange the circled letters to form the surprise answer, as suggested by the above cartoon.

Print answer here

JUMBLE®

Unscramble these four Jumbles, one letter
to each square, to form four ordinary words.

VOIDE

UISET

VELTEW

RHHUCC

We hear
you're the
best. Can you
help us find
the culprit?

I can start investi-
gating right away.
What's your
password?

It's
"password."

TO FIND OUT WHO HACKED
ITS EMAIL SERVER, THE
COMPANY HIRED A ---

Now arrange the circled letters to form
the surprise answer, as suggested by the
above cartoon.

Print
answer
here

" ⬚⬚ - ⬚⬚⬚⬚ - ⬚⬚⬚⬚ "

JUMBLE®

Unscramble these four Jumbles, one letter to each square, to form four ordinary words.

BAUTO

WEELJ

MARCOL

IPAMRI

I think I finally figured it out!

I saw her look up the answer online!

I figured it out in 10 seconds.

THE CAJUN CHEF WHO OVERSOLD HER ABILITY TO SOLVE THE "PUNNY" PUZZLE WAS A ———

Now arrange the circled letters to form the surprise answer, as suggested by the above cartoon.

Print answer here

" ⬡⬡⬡⬡⬡⬡ - ⬡⬡⬡⬡ "

JUMBLE®

Unscramble these four Jumbles, one letter to each square, to form four ordinary words.

PURTE

ARWEF

PLUSTC

GAVEOY

You really need to get it over the net. Also, the rules say you need to stand behind the line.

IF A TENNIS PLAYER IS GOING TO WIN CONSISTENTLY, HE OR SHE CAN'T HAVE A ----

Now arrange the circled letters to form the surprise answer, as suggested by the above cartoon.

Print answer here

JUMBLE®

Unscramble these four Jumbles, one letter to each square, to form four ordinary words.

EKROJ

SINBO

FAYRTD

DOYBNO

I'd love a lifetime contract.

You're teriffic! What kind of deal can we do?

WHEN THEY HIRED HIM AS THE NEW TIGHTROPE WALKER, HE HOPED IT WOULD BE A ---

Now arrange the circled letters to form the surprise answer, as suggested by the above cartoon.

Print answer here

JUMBLE

Unscramble these four Jumbles, one letter
to each square, to form four ordinary words.

TUTNY

LASIA

BOLBEB

MASCUP

I was just told this party has 1,000 kids coming, not 100. Can I get everything you have?

Of course!

WHEN THE CLOWN ASKED TO
PURCHASE THE STORE'S
ENTIRE INVENTORY, THE
OWNER SAID ---

Now arrange the circled letters to form
the surprise answer, as suggested by the
above cartoon.

Print answer here

" ⬡⬡⬡ " ⬡⬡⬡   ⬡⬡⬡⬡⬡⬡

JUMBLE®

Unscramble these four Jumbles, one letter to each square, to form four ordinary words.

SHECS

NUDOW

ROWNDA

ITAXFE

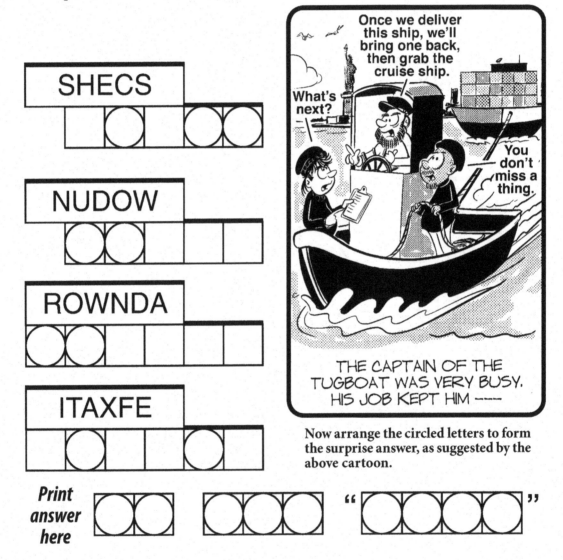

Once we deliver this ship, we'll bring one back, then grab the cruise ship.

What's next?

You don't miss a thing.

THE CAPTAIN OF THE TUGBOAT WAS VERY BUSY. HIS JOB KEPT HIM ----

Now arrange the circled letters to form the surprise answer, as suggested by the above cartoon.

Print answer here

"   "

JUMBLE®

Unscramble these four Jumbles, one letter
to each square, to form four ordinary words.

TAIRO

ASTEE

WERFUC

COLISA

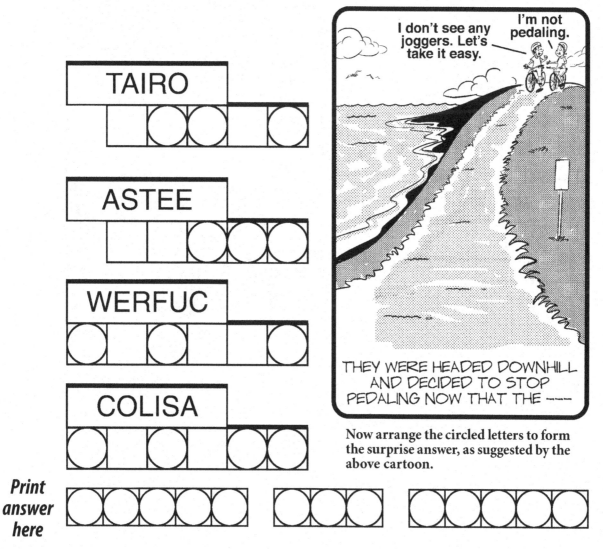

I don't see any joggers. Let's take it easy.

I'm not pedaling.

THEY WERE HEADED DOWNHILL
AND DECIDED TO STOP
PEDALING NOW THAT THE ----

Now arrange the circled letters to form
the surprise answer, as suggested by the
above cartoon.

**Print
answer
here**

JUMBLE®

Unscramble these four Jumbles, one letter to each square, to form four ordinary words.

SAREO

NATDS

CITYMS

QEOAPU

It started with 20 floors, then 10 more were added, then another 20.

Wow!

THE HISTORIC HIGH-RISE HAD A ----

Now arrange the circled letters to form the surprise answer, as suggested by the above cartoon.

Print answer here

JUMBLE®

Unscramble these four Jumbles, one letter to each square, to form four ordinary words.

KNAPR

RHIDT

ARKTEA

SLOYCT

She broke my mother's punch bowl!

Who invited her?

DON'T DRINK TOO MUCH ON NEW YEAR'S EVE! YOU DON'T WANT TO BE A ---

Now arrange the circled letters to form the surprise answer, as suggested by the above cartoon.

Print answer here

JUMBLE®

Unscramble these four Jumbles, one letter to each square, to form four ordinary words.

FIDUL

RPUNS

FIMSTI

PEDARA

I thought I asked you to clear this!

I was going to, but then the game came on.

HE PROMISED HER HE'D SHOVEL AND SALT THE WALKWAY, BUT IT ---

Now arrange the circled letters to form the surprise answer, as suggested by the above cartoon.

Print answer here

⬡⬡⬡⬡⬡⬡⬡ **HIS** ⬡⬡⬡⬡

162

JUMBLE®

Unscramble these six Jumbles, one letter to each square, to form six ordinary words.

GOIBLE

SLUIBY

KINNAP

CHYSIP

BERKAM

COATIN

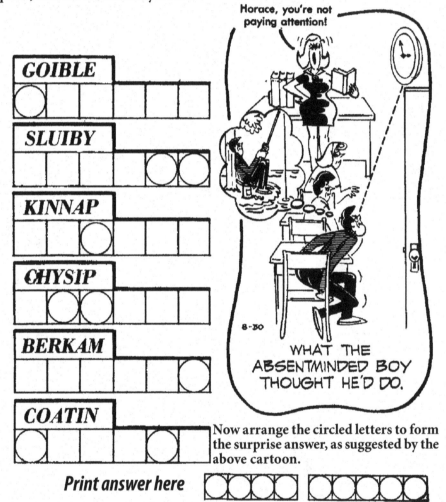

Horace, you're not paying attention!

8-30

WHAT THE ABSENTMINDED BOY THOUGHT HE'D DO.

Now arrange the circled letters to form the surprise answer, as suggested by the above cartoon.

Print answer here

164

JUMBLE®

Unscramble these six Jumbles, one letter to each square, to form six ordinary words.

BELFEE

CEADDE

PLOUCE

TRYPAN

HORTEY

SAHDIR

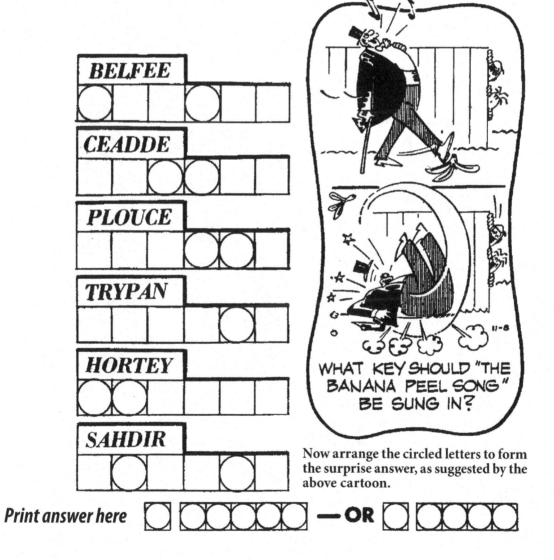

WHAT KEY SHOULD "THE BANANA PEEL SONG" BE SUNG IN?

Now arrange the circled letters to form the surprise answer, as suggested by the above cartoon.

Print answer here ☐ ☐☐☐☐☐ —**OR** ☐ ☐☐☐☐

JUMBLE®

Unscramble these six Jumbles, one letter
to each square, to form six ordinary words.

VYCOON

FESTOF

USDABE

VERDIF

NUIRJY

BIGTLE

Why is she
marrying an
officer?

Now arrange the circled letters to form
the surprise answer, as suggested by the
above cartoon.

Print
answer
here

"HE MADE A ⬡⬡⬡⬡ ⬡⬡⬡⬡⬡, ⬡⬡⬡!"

JUMBLE®

Unscramble these six Jumbles, one letter to each square, to form six ordinary words.

VEELEN

TRAULB

DINGHI

SHUBAM

UNDIPT

NECNAD

What about your diet?

HE BLUSHED RIGHT DOWN TO HIS FINGERTIPS BECAUSE HE WAS THIS.

Now arrange the circled letters to form the surprise answer, as suggested by the above cartoon.

Print answer here

JUMBLE®

Unscramble these six Jumbles, one letter
to each square, to form six ordinary words.

LUFNIX

RALLUP

ENDTOE

CLEBUK

WEGNIT

UNROAD

11-7

THIS VESSEL CONTAINS
JUST A LITTLE MORE
THAN FOUR QUARTS.

Now arrange the circled letters to form
the surprise answer, as suggested by the
above cartoon.

Print answer here A " ⬡⬡⬡⬡ - ⬡ - ⬡⬡ "

JUMBLE®

Unscramble these six Jumbles, one letter to each square, to form six ordinary words.

TRUFUE

ENGOUL

YATUBE

FLADGY

SENFUI

RUBBUS

Hurry there are more shops ahead

WHAT BUSY LADIES DID DURING THE VICTORIAN ERA.

Now arrange the circled letters to form the surprise answer, as suggested by the above cartoon.

Print answer here

" ⃝⃝⃝⃝⃝⃝⃝ " ⃝⃝⃝⃝⃝

JUMBLE®

Unscramble these six Jumbles, one letter to each square, to form six ordinary words.

CAMINA

CLARIA

SOPHIL

SIFUNE

GARNAL

GLOBIE

That was lovely

Do we have to go down?

WHAT THE BLUE NOSES BECAME WHEN THEY SCALED THE MOUNTAIN.

Now arrange the circled letters to form the surprise answer, as suggested by the above cartoon.

Print answer here

" ◯◯◯◯◯◯◯ " ◯◯◯◯◯◯◯◯◯

170

JUMBLE

Unscramble these six Jumbles, one letter to each square, to form six ordinary words.

UTTOWI

BAACAN

DRUGIT

FIMFUN

LIMBEN

MALBEC

You don't have the spark to succeed

HE GOT FIRED BECAUSE THE BOSS SAID HE LACKED ---

Now arrange the circled letters to form the surprise answer, as suggested by the above cartoon.

Print answer here

A " ◯◯◯◯◯◯◯ " ◯◯◯◯◯◯◯◯◯

JUMBLE®

Unscramble these six Jumbles, one letter to each square, to form six ordinary words.

DMAAMN

EVILAB

YIQUET

QUINUE

MADAKS

BURBYG

Come with me, sir

ELECTRONICS

½

THE SHOPLIFTER WAS CAUGHT BECAUSE HE HAD A ---

Now arrange the circled letters to form the surprise answer, as suggested by the above cartoon.

Print answer here

JUMBLE

Unscramble these six Jumbles, one letter
to each square, to form six ordinary words.

INGROI

OFTROG

GIBNEN

GRAIND

YEUFLE

ZEBRAL

This makes
it look
more elegant

WHAT THE SHOPPER
CONSIDERED THE
BORDER ON THE
TABLECLOTH.

Now arrange the circled letters to form
the surprise answer, as suggested by the
above cartoon.

Print answer here

A " ⬡⬡⬡⬡⬡⬡⬡ " ⬡⬡⬡⬡⬡⬡⬡⬡

JUMBLE®

Unscramble these six Jumbles, one letter to each square, to form six ordinary words.

AXELEH

TUBGED

GINNNI

DISUTO

SONIPO

REFTER

So, what do you think started it, Inspector?

It was definitely electrical, not gas that started this.

TO FIGURE OUT HOW THE BUSINESS BURNED DOWN, THEY NEEDED A ---

Now arrange the circled letters to form the surprise answer, as suggested by the above cartoon.

Print answer here

◯◯◯◯ " ◯◯◯◯◯◯◯◯◯◯◯◯◯◯◯◯◯ "

JUMBLE®

Unscramble these six Jumbles, one letter to each square, to form six ordinary words.

GROTEF

VIETNA

OSPEPO

SIRSIC

PEMIRR

JIRENU

THE BREAD COMPANY HOPED ITS NEW DOUGH RECIPE WOULD RESULT IN ----

Now arrange the circled letters to form the surprise answer, as suggested by the above cartoon.

Print answer here

JUMBLE®

Unscramble these six Jumbles, one letter to each square, to form six ordinary words.

HILCNF

CNITEE

CREADA

LAWESE

GRECAH

BRYDIH

WHEN LOUIE PASSED OUT CHECKS TO THE DRIVERS ON "TAXI," HE WAS GIVING EVERYONE ----

Now arrange the circled letters to form the surprise answer, as suggested by the above cartoon.

Print answer here

◯◯◯◯◯ " ◯◯◯◯ " ◯◯◯◯◯

176

JUMBLE®

Unscramble these six Jumbles, one letter to each square, to form six ordinary words.

CRETKO

DOUMIP

FONMIR

SNITIS

TORYPE

MALSUY

If we don't have houses to sell, I can't make any money.

Welcome Home Realty

House Listings

I'm afraid I will have to close.

IN
OUT

11/16

WHEN THE REAL ESTATE AGENT COULDN'T GET ENOUGH CLIENTS, SHE WAS ----

Now arrange the circled letters to form the surprise answer, as suggested by the above cartoon.

Print answer here

JUMBLE®

Unscramble these six Jumbles, one letter to each square, to form six ordinary words.

MUTANU

KESTAG

BLOGON

VEWLIS

LEHAWI

TIREDV

This is a disaster.

Everyone is at the beach.

THE WATER PARK HAD TO GO OUT OF BUSINESS BECAUSE NOT ENOUGH PEOPLE ----

Now arrange the circled letters to form the surprise answer, as suggested by the above cartoon.

Print answer here

178

JUMBLE®

Unscramble these six Jumbles, one letter to each square, to form six ordinary words.

TREETL

GREEEM

FARDIT

NAPUTE

HEELAX

YINREW

Wow! It's so huge!

It's so real!

THE MONSTER MOVIE ABOUT THE GIANT CYCLOPS WAS PLAYING AT THE ----

Now arrange the circled letters to form the surprise answer, as suggested by the above cartoon.

Print answer here

" ☐☐☐ " - ☐☐☐   ☐☐☐☐☐☐☐☐

JUMBLE

Unscramble these six Jumbles, one letter to each square, to form six ordinary words.

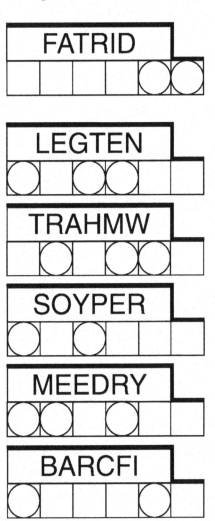

FATRID

LEGTEN

TRAHMW

SOYPER

MEEDRY

BARCFI

If you're saying that I get one million dollars whether I set the record or not, I'm in!

That's right! If you jump, you'll get it.

THE DAREDEVIL WOULD TRY TO BREAK THE WORLD RECORD AFTER GETTING THE ----

Now arrange the circled letters to form the surprise answer, as suggested by the above cartoon.

Print answer here

180

JUMBLE®

Unscramble these six Jumbles, one letter to each square, to form six ordinary words.

RASLIP

NEXYOG

ACTNAV

FUNXIL

ANGEEG

TOSHOE

Shouldn't they be doing homework or their chores?

This has to stop. They're turning into zombies.

5/31

AFTER INCREASING THEIR HOME'S BANDWIDTH, THEY WERE WORRIED ABOUT THEIR KIDS' ——

Now arrange the circled letters to form the surprise answer, as suggested by the above cartoon.

Print answer here

" "

JUMBLE®

Unscramble these six Jumbles, one letter to each square, to form six ordinary words.

SNOGRT

FOTINY

DARIHO

VECIED

MONICE

FPLOYP

I feel much better. I'm ready now for the week ahead.

I'm still on Rome time. I need some more rest.

7/12

IT WAS TIME FOR HER TO GET OUT OF BED BECAUSE SHE WAS ---

Now arrange the circled letters to form the surprise answer, as suggested by the above cartoon.

Print answer here

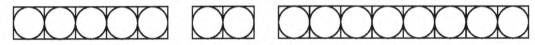

JUMBLE®

Unscramble these six Jumbles, one letter to each square, to form six ordinary words.

DEAFRO

DISOTU

LLOGAB

RULHOY

NINDAL

BELEFE

What should we do?

I think it's time for us to head on out.

10/11

THE SEAGULLS IN THE FLOCK ENJOYED THEIR TIME TOGETHER BECAUSE THEY WERE ----

Now arrange the circled letters to form the surprise answer, as suggested by the above cartoon.

Print answer here

183

Answers

1. **Jumbles:** STOOP BRIBE DRAGON SURTAX
Answer: Dipping your bread into gravy may be bad manners—but it's certainly also this—"GOOD TASTE"

2. **Jumbles:** ARRAY GAVEL EMBODY VERSUS
Answer: A man who claims he never makes a mistake isn't this—VERY BUSY

3. **Jumbles:** TEMPO ABATE GUITAR SPLEEN
Answer: A bikini never attracts attention until someone does this—PUTS IT ON

4. **Jumbles:** GOOSE AMUSE SAVORY BUSHEL
Answer: In these very words he told his wife who the boss was—"YOU'RE THE BOSS!"

5. **Jumbles:** AUDIT DECRY ENMITY BARROW
Answer: That lonely guy robbed a bank just so he could feel this—"WANTED"

6. **Jumbles:** GUMBO BRIAR FORKED CROTCH
Answer: She can dish it out, but can she do this?—COOK IT

7. **Jumbles:** MIDGE AUGUR DISCUS GENTLE
Answer: When they reach middle age, many people are reduced to this—REDUCING

8. **Jumbles:** COUCH ANKLE NUTRIA DEVOUR
Answer: The best way to tell a woman's age is when she's this—NOT AROUND

9. **Jumbles:** DUMPY HENCE RUBBER FORGET
Answer: The restaurant across from the theater was always packed because the play was strictly this—"FROM HUNGER"

10. **Jumbles:** BLOOM OFTEN ABSURD LEGUME
Answer: What kind of personality did that champion fencer have?—A "DUEL" ONE

11. **Jumbles:** FINAL MOOSE HEALTH FONDLY
Answer: What a man in love sometimes shows great ingenuity in making—A FOOL OF HIMSELF

12. **Jumbles:** BROOK DADDY ADROIT MEASLY
Answer: That beloved movie villain was so good at being this—SO BAD

13. **Jumbles:** CYNIC FAMED BARREL ABRUPT
Answer: How the backseat driver's husband drove—BY EAR

14. **Jumbles:** ASSAY LUNGE HINDER SPEEDY
Answer: Rich food, like destiny, can do this—SHAPE OUR ENDS

15. **Jumbles:** FLOOD TITLE SUBDUE JANGLE
Answer: How to assure that you don't lose money at the track—JUST DON'T GO

16. **Jumbles:** AWASH FAITH POPLIN SOCKET
Answer: Rich relatives left him a yacht, and ever since he's been talking about this—HIS "KIN SHIP"

17. **Jumbles:** FUNNY BUMPY REBUKE TROPHY
Answer: What happened when nylon stockings were first introduced?—THERE WAS A "RUN" ON THEM

18. **Jumbles:** TANGY PANDA REFUGE UPROAR
Answer: A good hamburger is made from this—THE GROUND UP

19. **Jumbles:** IDIOT BOUND PSYCHE FATHOM
Answer: What that graduation picture was—A PHOTO FINISH

20. **Jumbles:** NERVY CAMEO BEWARE MISHAP
Answer: When prices "soar"—SO ARE WE (sore)

21. **Jumbles:** SWAMP ENEMY CHALET PONCHO
Answer: "There's a strange drip in the basement. Shall I call the plumber?"—"NO, THE COPS"

22. **Jumbles:** PRIZE DRONE SCARCE DAMASK
Answer: A person of good judgment knows when to speak his mind and when to do this—MIND HOW HE SPEAKS

23. **Jumbles:** BAKED CANAL PODIUM NOGGIN
Answer: What the job of delivering parcels sometimes is—A BANG-UP ONE

24. **Jumbles:** WHISK COUGH GENTRY UNHOOK
Answer: In order to please his wife, he reluctantly agreed to go there—OUT OF HIS "WEIGH"

25. **Jumbles:** HIKER MADLY CANKER BABIED
Answer: The acrobat was the only guy who knew how to talk about himself—BEHIND HIS OWN BACK

26. **Jumbles:** SCARY FRIAR BLUISH RAVAGE
Answer: What came between those two poets turned professional boxers?—VERSUS

27. **Jumbles:** SLANT MERGE RAREFY ZODIAC
Answer: Another name for nostalgia—"YESTERDAZE"

28. **Jumbles:** AWOKE PILOT VORTEX DENOTE
Answer: He couldn't swim a stroke, but he knew this—EVERY "DIVE" IN TOWN

29. **Jumbles:** PIECE SANDY KINGLY ENCAMP
Answer: Their kid's college education seemed to be just this—PIGSKIN DEEP

30. **Jumbles:** LINEN ANNUL ENCORE HANSOM
Answer: What that blackguard was—A HEEL WITHOUT A "SOLE"

31. **Jumbles:** TWINE CHICK INFIRM BEHELD
Answer: She went to some length to change this—HER WIDTH

32. **Jumbles:** AFIRE PIANO ZIGZAG FOMENT
Answer: Like a ship, some speakers toot loudest when they're this—IN A FOG

33. **Jumbles:** ODDLY TOKEN CONVEX INLAID
Answer: Why the jury asked to see the accused safecracker again—THEY WERE DEAD "LOCKED"

34. **Jumbles:** RUMMY MONEY GIBBET HUNTER
Answer: What might Tom do when his car breaks down?—TOM "THUMB"

35. **Jumbles:** TOOTH DIZZY BOBBIN ICEBOX
Answer: An "addiction" to this can cause some people to become sleepy—"DICTION"

36. **Jumbles:** MESSY VIRUS HOOKED SCRIBE
Answer: What that amorous pitcher knew how to throw best—KISSES

37. **Jumbles:** FENCE PRIME GOATEE NOODLE
Answer: What might go on inside a compass?—"NEEDLE POINT"

38. **Jumbles:** POPPY MOUSE KISMET UNCURL
Answer: He was so dull that every time he left—THE ROOM LIT UP

39. **Jumbles:** KEYED HOUSE EXCITE PURIFY
Answer: Her appeal sprang from this—HER "EYE CUE"

40. **Jumbles:** ABIDE DUCAT POORLY BECKON
Answer: What the skeptic's outlook is—A "DOUBT LOOK"

41. **Jumbles:** OBESE USURY FLIMSY BUSILY
Answer: The only sure way of catching the next train is to—MISS THE ONE BEFORE

42. **Jumbles:** CURVE BELLE VOYAGE SHADOW
Answer: What a filibustering politician should do—"HALVE" HIS SAY

43. **Jumbles:** MOURN REBEL BALSAM DELUXE
Answer: That exotic perfume held her—"SMELL BOUND"

44. **Jumbles:** EIGHT STOIC HEAVEN TINGLE
Answer: A horse is what more people bet on—THAN GET ON

45. **Jumbles:** SWASH CLOTH DEVOUR GALLEY
Answer: In the real estate business one learns that the best investment on earth is usually this—EARTH

46. **Jumbles:** THINK ARRAY BETRAY MYSELF
Answer: The worst fault of an indiscreet guy is telling other people—THEIRS

47. **Jumbles:** KNOWN AWFUL LAYOFF MAKEUP
Answer: He found it easier to sit tight than this—WALK THAT WAY

48. **Jumbles:** VYING DEMON RATIFY TREATY
Answer: That spoiled kid would rather cry and get it than—TRY AND GET IT

49. **Jumbles:** ORBIT BLOOM TONGUE LEEWAY
Answer: Their old man made money in questionable ways, and now they're enjoying this—"WILL-GOTTEN" GAINS

50. **Jumbles:** PRUNE FETID STICKY EXPOSE
Answer: What a smuggler doesn't have—A SENSE OF DUTY

51. **Jumbles:** CLUCK LYRIC GROTTO SURELY
Answer: The kind of wrench he used to loosen the pipe—"SOCK-IT"

52. **Jumbles:** WAFER CRUSH HOOKUP COBALT
Answer: What the entrepreneur on the hunt was after—A FAST BUCK

53. **Jumbles:** GUMBO APPLY GADFLY BOUGHT
Answer: What the students studied at the mall—"BUY"-OLOGY

54. **Jumbles:** BANAL COLON SPLEEN IMBUED
Answer: What did the janitor do when he won the lottery?—HE CLEANED UP

55. **Jumbles:** SINGE FLORA ENTIRE SYMBOL
Answer: When his coffee was served cold it left him—BOILING

56. **Jumbles:** FRIAR CRAWL FRUGAL PARLOR
Answer: The beautician who gives permanents is called this—A CURL GIRL

57. **Jumbles:** PIOUS SIXTY PELVIS OUTCRY
Answer: What the shoe repair man was to his family—THEIR "SOLE" SUPPORT

58. **Jumbles:** LLAMA LINEN GIBBON CAUCUS
Answer: What the prisoners played in the exercise yard—CON GAMES

59. **Jumbles:** ACRID REBEL FLORID SUNDAE
Answer: What she wanted the talkative saleslady to do—PUT THE "LID" ON

60. **Jumbles:** SLANT DRONE JAILED REBUKE
Answer: Where the trash collector put his money—IN JUNK BONDS

61. **Jumbles:** ALIAS CLOAK CHORUS GENTLE
Answer: To the shoplifter the below-cost clothing was this—A REAL STEAL

62. **Jumbles:** DUCAT YOUNG FICKLE JUNIOR
Answer: A sporting event can cause this—"GRID" LOCK

63. **Jumbles:** MAXIM DUSKY MIDWAY KETTLE
Answer: The embezzler's favorite morning drink—"SKIMMED" MILK

64. **Jumbles:** EIGHT ADMIT BLEACH IMPEND
Answer: What their baby did to the new parents—"CHANGED" THEM

65. **Jumbles:** AXIOM MOUND ABLAZE CAUGHT
Answer: What a prizefighter's daily routine includes—BOX, LUNCH

66. **Jumbles:** BASIC RANCH ARCADE CANKER
Answer: How the detective solved the mystery—HE CRACKED THE CASE

67. **Jumbles:** TULIP BEGUN CAVORT INDOOR
Answer: When they learned about the star getting that coveted role, they—GOT THE PICTURE

68. **Jumbles:** GRIMY CRAFT OMELET FAMISH
Answer: What some take when they go shopping—THEIR TIME

69. **Jumbles:** THYME ABHOR IMPUGN RADISH
Answer: What the tallest player gave his coach—HIGH HOPES

70. **Jumbles:** LOVER PROBE FORKED LIKELY
Answer: What the accountant turned librarian remained—A BOOKKEEPER

71. **Jumbles:** EVOKE TEPID HANDED VASSAL
Answer: Some football players use a pigskin to get this—A SHEEPSKIN

72. **Jumbles:** GLOAT SNORT CARPET URCHIN
Answer: How the skinflints ended up after happy hour—AS "TIGHT" PALS

73. **Jumbles:** AVAIL FANCY DOUBLE TACKLE
Answer: The tightrope walker got into trouble because he had a—LACK OF BALANCE

74. **Jumbles:** AWARD ENTRY CANINE BEATEN
Answer: What the singer found when he became a cop—A NEW BEAT

75. **Jumbles:** MINOR DOUSE HAIRDO SHERRY
Answer: What the janitor always kept at arm's length—HIS HANDS

76. **Jumbles:** PARCH PAPER HOURLY CLAUSE
Answer: How she described her well-behaved young dog—A HUSH PUPPY

77. **Jumbles:** NEWLY SMOKY CRAVAT GUITAR
Answer: What they became when the insects attacked—THE SWAT TEAM

78. **Jumbles:** LAUGH AFOOT ARCTIC ORPHAN
Answer: What can be found in a sauna—A LOT OF HOT AIR

79. **Jumbles:** CRAZE GUEST BOTANY DELUGE
Answer: What the pilot ran into when the flight was late—TURBULENCE

80. **Jumbles:** ADULT FAULT DEMISE PESTLE
Answer: A facelift that doesn't cost a penny—A SMILE

81. **Jumbles:** HUMID ANKLE URCHIN FEDORA
Answer: The trail through the swamp caused the cross-country race to—RUN "A-MUCK"

82. **Jumbles:** OPERA SPENT OPPOSE SPRUCE
Answer: Whether or not the coin would land heads or tails was—A TOSS UP

83. **Jumbles:** CRYPT MADLY MEDLEY APPEAR
Answer: She though the new glasses were—"EYE-DEAL"

84. **Jumbles:** HASTY DUNCE TUMBLE ALWAYS
Answer: The garbage dump turned the landscape into a—WASTELAND

85. **Jumbles:** YUCKY ABIDE HUNGRY SCROLL
Answer: The shrubs needed trimming because they were too—BUSHY

86. **Jumbles:** FLINT BURST EASILY OPPOSE
Answer: Casper bought a cabin in the woods so that he could live in the—"BOO-NIES"

87. **Jumbles:** QUOTA TWINE DISOWN UNFOLD
Answer: When the bottled water company went bankrupt, its stock was—LIQUIDATED

88. **Jumbles:** RIGID FRAUD FINISH EATERY
Answer: King Kong attended Yankees games because he was a—HUGE FAN

89. **Jumbles:** VIDEO BLIND MINGLE SAILOR
Answer: After working all day at the funeral home, he was happy to get back to his—LIVING ROOM

90. **Jumbles:** METAL SILKY DRENCH WINERY
Answer: After getting sick Friday, on Saturday, she was—WEAKENED

91. **Jumbles:** GRAPH KITTY CUSTOM ENGULF
Answer: After buying shares in a company that went bankrupt the next day, the broker was a—LAUGHING STOCK

92. **Jumbles:** AGILE ELOPE ANYHOW SYRUPY
Answer: When the king needed to go to the hospital, it was a—ROYAL PAIN

93. **Jumbles:** COUCH BURLY ALLEGE BISECT
Answer: Their breakfast by the water included—BAY GULLS

94. **Jumbles:** ACUTE PESKY AMAZED PROPER
Answer: The shoppers thought the new grocery store was—A SUPER MARKET

95. **Jumbles:** DAZED EAGLE GROUND HIDDEN
Answer: The night watchman, viewing the basketball game on TV, particularly liked all the—GUARDING

96. **Jumbles:** AROMA PRINT DECODE POLLEN
Answer: To get their fancy new church spire, they—PAID TOP DOLLAR

97. **Jumbles:** FRAUD LEAKY SWIVEL BECAME
Answer: After losing the game, the bridge partners—BID FAREWELL

98. **Jumbles:** CHIRP PROBE MUTTER ASSURE
Answer: The Santa Monica beach sea gull was experiencing—"PIER" PRESSURE

99. **Jumbles:** JOUST CEASE ACCESS BOXCAR
Answer: He didn't want to talk about his wrestling match loss because it was a—SORE SUBJECT

100. **Jumbles:** BYLAW TALLY DRAFTY FRENZY
Answer: When she saw the fancy new café that served Earl Grey and Chai, she thought—"LA-TEA-DA"

101. **Jumbles:** DRESS UNFIT DEGREE ABSORB
Answer: He asked if the mattress came with a warranty, and the salesman told him he could—REST ASSURED

102. **Jumbles:** TINGLE VOICE APPEAR SHADOW
Answer: He poked his skeptical buddy with the new spear to—PROVE HIS POINT

103. **Jumbles:** ABHOR GRILL INHALE UTMOST
Answer: When the machinery at the lumber factory broke down, everyone was—MILLING ABOUT

104. **Jumbles:** HOIST HEDGE MARKET DEFUSE
Answer: After throwing the touchdown pass to win the game, his teammates—RUSHED HIM

105. **Jumbles:** DECAY BRISK STRAND WANTED
Answer: The internet site that sold discount wedding gowns had a—WEB AD-DRESS

106. **Jumbles:** MIMIC ADAGE SORROW POETRY
Answer: When the author went for a horseback ride, he ended up getting—"RIDER'S" CRAMP

107. **Jumbles:** CHEEK AMAZE DREAMY OPPOSE
Answer: After the pit stop, the race car—RE-ZOOMED

108. **Jumbles:** DINKY ISSUE INVERT EFFORT
Answer: The identical twins were just alike, even when they were—INDIFFERENT

109. **Jumbles:** UDDER TAUNT UNCORK CLIQUE
Answer: When the British noblemen got into an argument, they—DUKED IT OUT

110. **Jumbles:** SPENT ROBOT ACTIVE CLAMMY
Answer: James Bond complained about his drink because it was too—"MAR-TEENY"

111. **Jumbles:** IMPEL ALIKE CAUGHT ENTITY
Answer: After hunting all night, the wolves decided to—PACK IT IN

112. **Jumbles:** LIMIT HATCH CHEESY COUPON
Answer: The transmission mechanic came through—IN THE CLUTCH

113. **Jumbles:** MANLY DWELL FATTEN BIRDIE
Answer: When the scarecrows had an outing, they had a—FIELD DAY

114. **Jumbles:** CHAOS HARSH PIRACY HELMET
Answer: The bounty hunter's slogan was a—CATCHY PHRASE

115. **Jumbles:** MINCE GRAPH STRING ACCENT
Answer: When a lot of bouquets were needed, they made—ARRANGEMENTS

116. **Jumbles:** NEWLY ORBIT INJECT UNFOLD
Answer: The concert music was changed, but the musician hadn't been—"NOTE-IFIED"

117. **Jumbles:** LUNGE HAVOC PODIUM POETIC
Answer: Audiences love "Jurassic Park" and thought it was—"DINO-MIGHT"

118. **Jumbles:** SHAME TWICE RODENT PEACHY
Answer: The antisocial octopus welcomed the unexpected visitor—WITH OPEN ARMS

119. **Jumbles:** YUCKY TARDY FIXATE ABSURD
Answer: The calendar factory produced calendars—DAY AFTER DAY

120. **Jumbles:** The number that equals four plus four didn't exist until it was—"CRE-EIGHT-ED"

121. **Jumbles:** WHEAT BRINK CANCEL BRIGHT
Answer: She knew what two times two equaled and didn't have to—THINK TWICE

122. **Jumbles:** WOUND GIDDY STIGMA CATNIP
Answer: She threw out his old recliner and he wasn't going to take it—SITTING DOWN

123. **Jumbles:** WHARF PRONG ADJUST PULSAR
Answer: The atmosphere of Venus and Earth are—WORLDS APART

124. **Jumbles:** GUPPY CABIN MEMORY ROTATE
Answer: The farmer with all the junked cars on his land had a—BUMPER CROP

125. **Jumbles:** WEARY RIGID SYNTAX CAUGHT
Answer: What does your money become when you combine "THE" and "IRS"?—THEIRS

126. **Jumbles:** MANLY DITTO RIPSAW VOYAGE
Answer: Traffic on the horse farm was caused by—"TAIL-GAITERS"

127. **Jumbles:** DOILY BRAVE PILLOW SYMBOL
Answer: The alligator was stressed out because he was—SWAMPED

128. **Jumbles:** HANDY BOGUS VERIFY YONDER
Answer: When the group of friends took a photo together, they took a photo of—"EVERY-BUDDY"

129. **Jumbles:** GRILL ADOPT AFLOAT POUNCE
Answer: When Amundsen reached the bottom of the Earth in 1911, he put a—FLAG ON A POLE

130. **Jumbles:** DIVOT UNCAP FACTOR GENTLE
Answer: New at the bread company, he was often caught—LOAFING

131. **Jumbles:** CYNIC SPELL FRUGAL TIPTOE
Answer: There are more than 1,000 satellites orbiting Earth, because there's—PLENTY OF SPACE

132. **Jumbles:** CHAOS ELECT SORROW MONKEY
Answer: When the rancher's cattle escaped under the fence, he said—"HOLE-Y" COW

133. **Jumbles:** ENACT ORBIT MADCAP LUXURY
Answer: With each glass of wine they filled, money—POURED IN

134. **Jumbles:** IMAGE HARSH PROPER PRANCE
Answer: When the twins spoke at the same time, sometimes they would—"PAIR-A-PHRASE"

135. **Jumbles:** VOCAL TINGE INFORM SCRIBE
Answer: At the trial, the defendant avoided this by testifying with this—CONVICTION

136. **Jumbles:** FLUID FLOOD TORRID HAZARD
Answer: When the politicians went for a balloon ride, the balloon was—FULL OF HOT AIR

137. Jumbles: FEIGN ELUDE FEDORA ACCESS
Answer: The karate instructor installed his own wrought iron because he wanted—SELF "DE-FENCE"

138. Jumbles: HANDY AVAIL SPRING FLORAL
Answer: They hoped the chef would be a long-term hit, not just a—FLASH IN THE PAN

139. Jumbles: GRAVY INPUT SUPERB HAPPEN
Answer: The happy kitty was this type of cat—A "PURR-SIAN"

140. Jumbles: UNFIT NINTH AWHILE GLOSSY
Answer: Business at the new driving range was—IN FULL SWING

141. Jumbles: WEARY HUMID GLITCH BOUNTY
Answer: Darrin Stephens was instantly attracted to Samantha and found her—BEWITCHING

142. Jumbles: BULKY NEEDY FORGOT HOLLER
Answer: He hurried to second base because he wanted to get there—ON THE DOUBLE

143. Jumbles: UNCLE CABLE SIDING KNOTTY
Answer: He rode the mechanical bull because it was on his—"BUCK-IT" LIST

144. Jumbles: FLOWN HOLLY JACKET ATTAIN
Answer: When the mayor gave her annual speech, it was the—TALK OF THE TOWN

145. Jumbles: BRAVE KUDOS STENCH LEVITY
Answer: She wanted to drop science, but her parents advised her to—STAY THE COURSE

146. Jumbles: NINTH UPEND AFLOAT FIDDLE
Answer: Captain Hook wanted to capture Peter and the Lost Boys, but his plans—DIDN'T PAN OUT

147. Jumbles: PINCH SHAME DIVIDE TRAUMA
Answer: The ghost didn't have many friends because he was so—MEAN-SPIRITED

148. Jumbles: FLIRT FOCAL ODDEST WANTED
Answer: Voting allows you to make your voice heard, unless you—ELECT NOT TO

149. Jumbles: SHAKY ERUPT STRING OBLONG
Answer: The young men running indoors were disciplined for being too—"BOY-STEROUS"

150. Jumbles: WALTZ ARENA DAYBED COSMOS
Answer: When it came to money, the successful shrimp company—MADE BOATLOADS

151. Jumbles: VIDEO SUITE TWELVE CHURCH
Answer: To find out who hacked its email server, the company hired a—"DE-TECH-TIVE"

152. Jumbles: ABOUT JEWEL CLAMOR IMPAIR
Answer: The Cajun chef who oversold her ability to solve the "punny" puzzle was a—"JUMBLE-LIAR"

153. Jumbles: ERUPT WAFER SCULPT VOYAGE
Answer: If a tennis player is going to win consistently, he or she can't have a—FAULTY SERVE

154. Jumbles: JOKER BISON DRAFTY NOBODY
Answer: When they hired him as the new tightrope walker, he hoped it would be a—STEADY JOB

155. Jumbles: NUTTY ALIAS BOBBLE CAMPUS
Answer: When the clown asked to purchase the store's entire inventory, the owner said—"BUY" ALL MEANS

156. Jumbles: CHESS WOUND ONWARD FIXATE
Answer: The captain of the tugboat was very busy. His job kept him—ON HIS "TOWS"

157. Jumbles: RATIO TEASE CURFEW SOCIAL
Answer: They were headed downhill and decided to stop pedaling now that the—COAST WAS CLEAR

158. Jumbles: AROSE STAND MYSTIC OPAQUE
Answer: The historic high-rise had a—STORIED PAST

159. Jumbles: PRANK THIRD KARATE COSTLY
Answer: Don't drink too much on New Year's Eve! You don't want to be a—PARTY CRASHER

160. Jumbles: FLUID SPURN MISFIT PARADE
Answer: He promised her he'd shovel and salt the walkway, but it—SLIPPED HIS MIND

161. Jumbles: OBLIGE BUSILY NAPKIN PHYSIC EMBARK ACTION
Answer: What the absentminded boy thought he'd do—PLAY HOOKY

162. Jumbles: FEEBLE DECADE COUPLE PANTRY THEORY RADISH
Answer: What key should "The Banana Peel Song" be sung in?—C SHARP OR B FLAT

163. Jumbles: CONVOY OFFSET ABUSED FERVID INJURY GIBLET
Answer: Why is she marrying an officer?—"HE MADE A GOOD OFFER, SIR!"

164. Jumbles: ELEVEN BRUTAL HIDING AMBUSH PUNDIT CANNED
Answer: He blushed right down to his fingertips because he was this—CAUGHT RED-HANDED

165. Jumbles: INFLUX PLURAL DENOTE BUCKLE TWINGE AROUND
Answer: This vessel contains just a little more than four quarts—A "GALL-E-ON"

166. Jumbles: FUTURE LOUNGE BEAUTY GADFLY INFUSE SUBURB
Answer: What busy ladies did during the Victorian era—"BUSTLED" ABOUT

167. Jumbles: MANIAC RACIAL POLISH INFUSE RAGLAN OBLIGE
Answer: What the blue noses became when they scaled the mountain—"SOCIAL" CLIMBERS

168. Jumbles: OUTWIT CABANA TURGID MUFFIN NIMBLE BECALM
Answer: He got fired because the boss said he lacked—A "BURNING" AMBITION

169. Jumbles: MADMAN VIABLE EQUITY UNIQUE DAMASK GRUBBY
Answer: The shoplifter was caught because he had a—BAD "TAKE-NIQUE"

170. Jumbles: ORIGIN FORGOT BENIGN DARING EYEFUL BLAZER
Answer: What the shopper considered the border on the tablecloth—A "FRINGE" BENEFIT

171. Jumbles: EXHALE BUDGET INNING STUDIO POISON FERRET
Answer: To figure out how the business burned down they needed a—FIRE "DISTINGUISHER"

172. Jumbles: FORGET NATIVE OPPOSE CRISIS PRIMER INJURE
Answer: The bread company hoped its new dough recipe would result in—RISING PROFITS

173. Jumbles: FLINCH ENTICE ARCADE WEASEL CHARGE HYBRID
Answer: When Louie passed out checks to the drivers on "Taxi," he was giving everyone—THEIR "FARE" SHARE

174. Jumbles: ROCKET PODIUM INFORM INSIST POETRY ASYLUM
Answer: When the real estate agent couldn't get enough clients, she was—OUT OF COMMISSION

175. Jumbles: AUTUMN GASKET OBLONG SWIVEL AWHILE DIVERT
Answer: The water park had to go out of business because not enough people—WENT DOWN THE TUBES

176. Jumbles: LETTER EMERGE ADRIFT PEANUT EXHALE WINERY
Answer: The monster movie about the giant cyclops was playing at the—"EYE"-MAX THEATER

177. Jumbles: ADRIFT GENTLE WARMTH OSPREY REMEDY FABRIC
Answer: The daredevil would try to break the world record after getting the—ATTEMPTING OFFER

178. Jumbles: SPIRAL OXYGEN VACANT INFLUX ENGAGE SOOTHE
Answer: After increasing their home's bandwidth, they were worried about their kids'—INTERNET "EXCESS"

179. Jumbles: STRONG NOTIFY HAIRDO DEVICE INCOME FLOPPY
Answer: It was time for her to get out of bed because she was—TIRED OF SLEEPING

180. Jumbles: FEDORA STUDIO GLOBAL HOURLY INLAND FEEBLE
Answer: The seagulls in the flock enjoyed their time together because they were—BIRDS OF A FEATHER

Need More Jumbles®?

Order any of these books through your bookseller or call Triumph Books toll-free at 800-888-4741.

Jumble® Books

More than 175 puzzles each!

Cowboy Jumble®
• ISBN: 978-1-62937-355-3

Jammin' Jumble®
• ISBN: 978-1-57243-844-6

Java Jumble®
• ISBN: 978-1-60078-415-6

Jet Set Jumble®
• ISBN: 978-1-60078-353-1

Jolly Jumble®
• ISBN: 978-1-60078-214-5

Jumble® Anniversary
• ISBN: 987-1-62937-734-6

Jumble® Ballet
• ISBN: 978-1-62937-616-5

Jumble® Birthday
• ISBN: 978-1-62937-652-3

Jumble® Celebration
• ISBN: 978-1-60078-134-6

Jumble® Champion
• ISBN: 978-1-62937-870-1

Jumble® Coronation
• ISBN: 978-1-62937-976-0

Jumble® Cuisine
• ISBN: 978-1-62937-735-3

Jumble® Drag Race
• ISBN: 978-1-62937-483-3

Jumble® Ever After
• ISBN: 978-1-62937-785-8

Jumble® Explorer
• ISBN: 978-1-60078-854-3

Jumble® Explosion
• ISBN: 978-1-60078-078-3

Jumble® Fever
• ISBN: 978-1-57243-593-3

Jumble® Galaxy
• ISBN: 978-1-60078-583-2

Jumble® Garden
• ISBN: 978-1-62937-653-0

Jumble® Genius
• ISBN: 978-1-57243-896-5

Jumble® Geography
• ISBN: 978-1-62937-615-8

Jumble® Getaway
• ISBN: 978-1-60078-547-4

Jumble® Gold
• ISBN: 978-1-62937-354-6

Jumble® Health
• ISBN: 978-1-63727-085-1

Jumble® Jackpot
• ISBN: 978-1-57243-897-2

Jumble® Jailbreak
• ISBN: 978-1-62937-002-6

Jumble® Jambalaya
• ISBN: 978-1-60078-294-7

Jumble® Jitterbug
• ISBN: 978-1-60078-584-9

Jumble® Journey
• ISBN: 978-1-62937-549-6

Jumble® Jubilation
• ISBN: 978-1-62937-784-1

Jumble® Jubilee
• ISBN: 978-1-57243-231-4

Jumble® Juggernaut
• ISBN: 978-1-60078-026-4

Jumble® Kingdom
• ISBN: 978-1-62937-079-8

Jumble® Knockout
• ISBN: 978-1-62937-078-1

Jumble® Madness
• ISBN: 978-1-892049-24-7

Jumble® Magic
• ISBN: 978-1-60078-795-9

Jumble® Mania
• ISBN: 978-1-57243-697-8

Jumble® Marathon
• ISBN: 978-1-60078-944-1

Jumble® Masterpiece
• ISBN: 978-1-62937-916-6

Jumble® Neighbor
• ISBN: 978-1-62937-845-9

Jumble® Parachute
• ISBN: 978-1-62937-548-9

Jumble® Party
• ISBN: 978-1-63727-008-0

Jumble® Safari
• ISBN: 978-1-60078-675-4

Jumble® Sensation
• ISBN: 978-1-60078-548-1

Jumble® Skyscraper
• ISBN: 978-1-62937-869-5

Jumble® Symphony
• ISBN: 978-1-62937-131-3

Jumble® Theater
• ISBN: 978-1-62937-484-0

Jumble® Time Machine: 1972
• ISBN: 978-1-63727-082-0

Jumble® Trouble
• ISBN: 978-1-62937-917-3

Jumble® University
• ISBN: 978-1-62937-001-9

Jumble® Unleashed
• ISBN: 978-1-62937-844-2

Jumble® Vacation
• ISBN: 978-1-60078-796-6

Jumble® Wedding
• ISBN: 978-1-62937-307-2

Jumble® Workout
• ISBN: 978-1-60078-943-4

Jump, Jive and Jumble®
• ISBN: 978-1-60078-215-2

Lunar Jumble®
• ISBN: 978-1-60078-853-6

Monster Jumble®
• ISBN: 978-1-62937-213-6

Mystic Jumble®
• ISBN: 978-1-62937-130-6

Rainy Day Jumble®
• ISBN: 978-1-60078-352-4

Royal Jumble®
• ISBN: 978-1-60078-738-6

Sports Jumble®
• ISBN: 978-1-57243-113-3

Summer Fun Jumble®
• ISBN: 978-1-57243-114-0

Touchdown Jumble®
• ISBN: 978-1-62937-212-9

Oversize Jumble® Books

More than 500 puzzles!

Colossal Jumble®
• ISBN: 978-1-57243-490-5

Jumbo Jumble®
• ISBN: 978-1-57243-314-4

Jumble® Crosswords™

More than 175 puzzles!

Jumble® Crosswords™
• ISBN: 978-1-57243-347-2